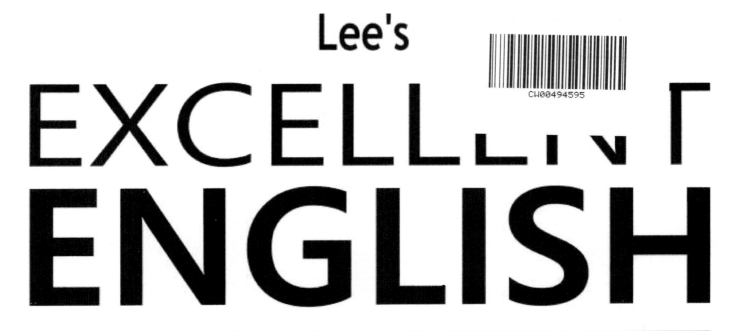

Lee's
EXCELLENT
ENGLISH

BEGINNER COURSE

Ukrainian Edition

Lee's Books

ISBN: 9798786723398

Contents

Lesson 1

- Learn the words
- Learn the sentences
- Learn the phonics
- Test yourself!

My pencil case

мій пенал

Learn the words

1. **a pencil**
   олівець

2. **an eraser**
   гумка

3. **some glue**
   клей

4. **a pencil sharpener**
   точилка

5. **some whiteout**
   коректор

6. **a pen**
   ручка

7. **a ruler**
   лінійка

8. **some tape**
   сантиметр

9. **a marker**
   маркер

10. **a crayon**
    кольоровий олівець

Write the missing letters!

1. p_ _c_ _

2. e_a_e_

3. g_ _ _

4. pe_c_l sh_r_ _n_ _

5. w_i_ _o_t

6. p_ _

7. r_ _ _r

8. t_ _ _

9. m_r_e_

10. c_a_o_

Have fun with the words!

Word Search

```
c e z c a p n g y j c t x m e m h k
z l y r r e m s d r d m a r k e r q
h u n a h n h h f i k i f v x u l j
u n w y p e n c i l e a j s n d o y
x q d o g c e r a s e r x b x a i o
f b h n w t n g w h i t e o u t h e
u o c v g t a k h c s r x v a h q y
f v u x l p c p v i g u u x m u q g
r c s c u a w f e b e l j d r o c x
z e p b e o j p k d p e b a z r h e
t c b y h a l k d k v r f z o a f l
w a p e n c i l s h a r p e n e r v
```

Words are hidden → ↓ and ↘ .

pencil sharpener

pen

marker

whiteout

crayon

ruler

tape

glue

pencil

eraser

What is this?

It is <u>a pencil</u>.

It is not <u>an eraser</u>.

What is that?

It is <u>a crayon</u>.

It is not <u>a marker</u>.

Write the missing words!

What _____ this?

It is a _____ sharpener.

It is _____ a _____ .

What _____ _____ ?

_____ is an _____ .

It _____ _____ a _____ .

What _____ this?

It _____ a _____ .

_____ is _____ _____ .

_____ ?

_____ .

_____ .

Is this a __marker__?

Yes, it is.

No, it is not.

Is that __whiteout__?

Yes, it is.

No, it is not.

Write the missing words!

Is this a _____?

Yes, it _____.

No, _____ is _____.

Is this _____ _____?

_____, it _____.

_____, it is _____.

Is _____ a _____?

Yes, _____.

No, _____.

_____?

_____.

_____.

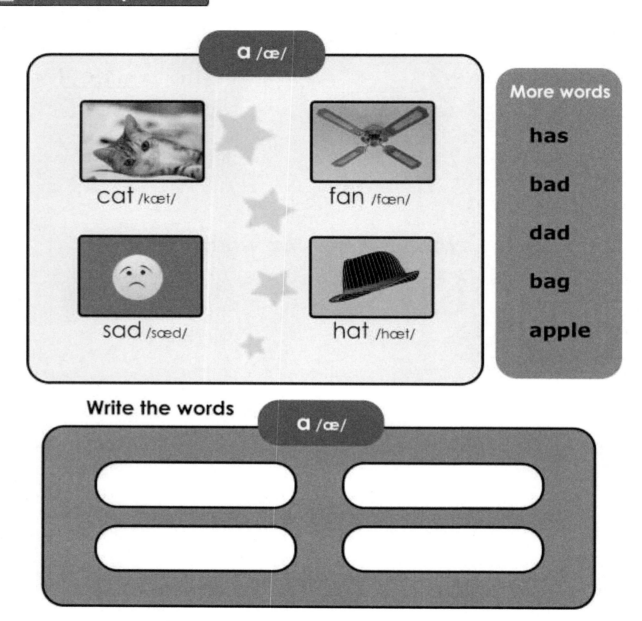

a /æ/

cat /kæt/

fan /fæn/

sad /sæd/

hat /hæt/

More words

has

bad

dad

bag

apple

Write the words

a /æ/

Write the letters & Read the sentences!

My d_d h_s a s_d c_t.

This h_t is b_d.

The _pple is in the b_g.

Complete the words

1. p_____l   3. m_____r   5. c_____n

2. t_____e   4. e_____r   6. w_____t

Write the answer next to the letter "A"

A: ___ **7.** ___ is ___ eraser.

a. This, a
b. they, an
c. It, an

A: ___ **8.** It ___ not a ___.

a. is, eraser
b. is, pencil sharpener
c. are, marker

A: ___ **9.** What is this? It is ___ tape.

a. a
b. an
c. x

A: ___ **10.** Is this ___? No, it ___.

a. pencil, is not
b. tape, is not
c. whiteout, not

Answers on Page 306

Lesson 2

- Learn the words
- Learn the sentences
- Learn the phonics
- Test yourself!

In the classroom

в класі

Learn the words

1. **chair**
стілець

2. **desk**
стіл

3. **blackboard**
класна дошка

4. **whiteboard**
біла дошка

5. **computer**
комп'ютер

6. **globe**
глобус

7. **clock**
годинник

8. **book**
книга

9. **bookshelf**
книжкова полиця

10. **poster**
плакат

Write the missing letters!

1. c_ _ _r

2. d_ _ _

3. bl_c_b_a_ _

4. w_it_b_a_d

5. _o_p_t_r

6. g_ _ _e

7. cl_c_

8. b_ _k

9. b_o_sh_l_

10. p_s_e_

Have fun with the words!

b l a c k b o a r d

1. desk
2. blackboard
3. computer
4. bookshelf
5. clock
6. whiteboard
7. poster
8. book
9. globe
10. chair

What are these?   What are those?

They are <u>chair</u>s.   They are <u>whiteboard</u>s.

They are not <u>desk</u>s.   They are not <u>blackboard</u>s.

Write the missing words!

What _____ these?

They are _____ .

They _____ _____ bookshelves.

What _____ those?

They _____ _____ .

They are _____ _____ .

What _____ _____ ?

_____ are _____ .

_____ _____ not _____ .

_____ ?

_____ .

_____ .

Are these <u>globe</u>s?   Are those <u>computer</u>s?

Yes, they are.   Yes, they are.

No, they are not.   No, they are not.

Write the missing words!

Are these _____?

Yes, they _____.

No, _____ are _____.

Are those _____?

_____, they _____.

_____, they are _____.

_____ these _____?

Yes, _____ _____.

No, _____ _____ _____.

_____?

_____.

_____.

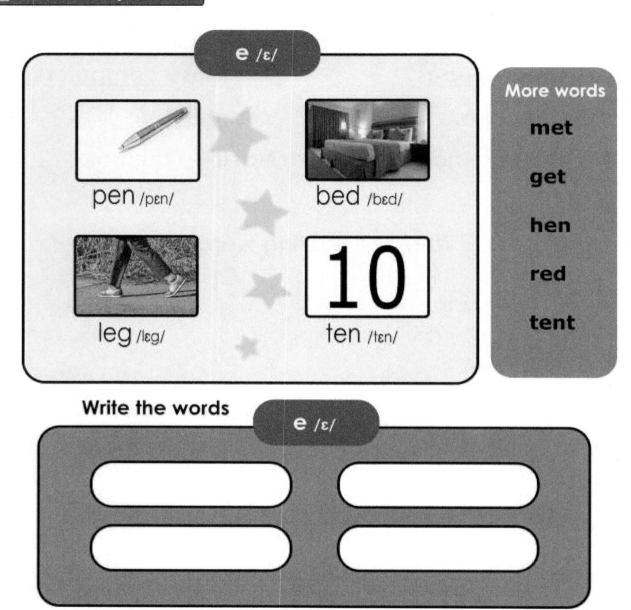

e /ɛ/

pen /pɛn/

bed /bɛd/

leg /lɛg/

10

ten /tɛn/

More words

met

get

hen

red

tent

Write the words

e /ɛ/

Write the letters & Read the sentences!

I will g_t a r_d p_n.

I see t_n h_ns in the t_nt.

T_d m_t K_n and Fr_d.

Complete the words

1. c_____r   3. p_____r   5. w_____d

2. g_____e   4. b_____f   6. d_____k

Write the answer next to the letter "A"

A: ___ **7.** They ___.

a. are bookshelves
b. is bookshelves
c. are bookshelfs

A: ___ **8.** What are these?

a. They are whiteboard.
b. They are whiteboards.
c. It is a whiteboard.

A: ___ **9.** Are these posters?

a. Yes, they is.
b. No, they are.
c. Yes, they are.

A: ___ **10.** Are those ___? Yes, they are.

a. books
b. blackboard
c. bookshelf

Answers on Page 306

Lesson 3

- Learn the words
- Learn the sentences
- Learn the phonics
- Test yourself!

Colors

кольори

Learn the words

1. **red**
червоний

2. **yellow**
жовтий

3. **green**
зелений

4. **blue**
синій

5. **purple**
фіолетовий

6. **orange**
помаранчевий

7. **brown**
коричневий

8. **pink**
рожевий

9. **black**
чорний

10. **white**
білий

Write the missing letters!

1. r_ _

2. y_ _l_w

3. g_e_n

4. b_u_

5. p_ _p_e

6. o_a_ _e

7. b_o_ _

8. p_ _ _

9. b_a_ _

10. w_i _ _

Have fun with the words!

Write the 3 missing words

1._____

2. _____

3. _____

green
red
blue
yellow
pink
black
orange

1._____

2. _____

3. _____

black
purple
yellow
white
brown
pink
blue

1._____

2. _____

3. _____

white
purple
orange
brown
red
black
green

1._____

2. _____

3. _____

orange
purple
white
green
pink
yellow
blue

1._____

2. _____

3. _____

purple
black
brown
green
orange
red
white

1._____

2. _____

3. _____

black
blue
brown
pink
yellow
red
green

What color is this?

It is <u>yellow</u>.

It isn't <u>green</u>.

What color is that?

It is <u>purple</u>.

It isn't <u>blue</u>.

Write the missing words!

What _____ is this?

It is _____ .

It _____ _____ .

What _____ _____ that?

It _____ _____ .

_____ isn't _____ .

_____ _____ _____ this?

_____ is _____ .

_____ _____ white.

_____ ?

_____ .

_____ .

Is this **pen** **red**?

Yes, it is.

No, it isn't. It is **brown**.

Is that **crayon** **pink**?

Yes, it is.

No, it isn't. It is **orange**.

Write the missing words!

Is this apple _____?

Yes, it _____.

No, it _____. It's _____.

Is _____ chair _____?

Yes, _____ is.

_____, it _____. It is _____.

_____ this _____ _____?

Yes, _____ _____.

No, _____ _____. It _____ _____.

_____?

_____.

_____.

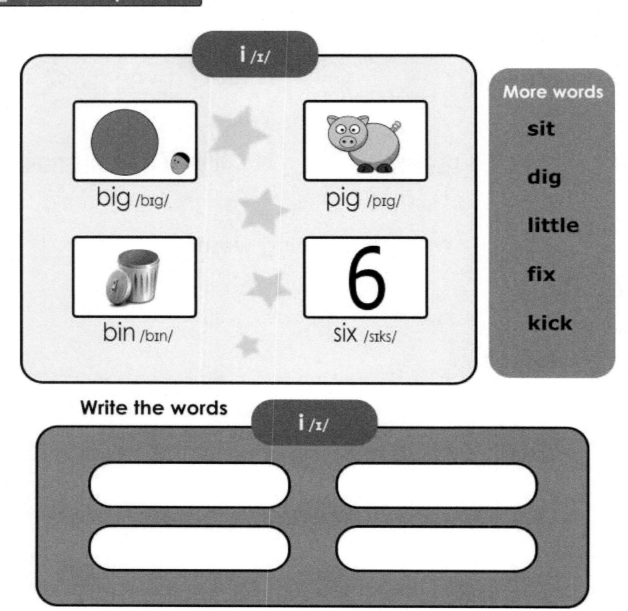

i /ɪ/

big /bɪg/

pig /pɪg/

bin /bɪn/

six /sɪks/

More words

sit

dig

little

fix

kick

Write the words

i /ɪ/

Write the letters & Read the sentences!

Th_s p_g _s b_g.

I f_x s_x b_ns.

I s_t on the l_ttle bench w_th h_m.

Complete the words

1. y_____w   3. o_____e   5. b_____k

2. b_____n   4. g_____n   6. p_____e

Write the answer next to the letter "A"

A: ___ **7.** What color ___?

a. is these
b. is this
c. are that

A: ___ **8.** What color is that?

a. It is a green.
b. Its purple.
c. It is blue.

A: ___ **9.** Is this pen blue?

a. Yes, it is.
b. Yes it is.
c. No, it is. It's red.

A: ___ **10.** Is that ___?

a. brown desk
b. desk brown
c. desks brown

Answers on Page 306

Lesson

4

- Learn the words
- Learn the sentences
- Learn the phonics
- Test yourself!

My family

моя родина

Learn the words

1. **grandmother**
   бабуся

2. **grandfather**
   дідусь

3. **baby sister**
   молодша сестра

4. **baby brother**
   молодший брат

5. **aunt**
   тітка

6. **uncle**
   дядько

7. **sister**
   сестра

8. **brother**
   брат

9. **mother**
   мати

10. **father**
    батько

Write the missing letters!

1. g_a_ _m_t_e_

2. g_a_df_ _h_ _

3. b_ _y s_s_ _r

4. b_b_ b_o_h_ _

5. a_n_

6. _n_ _e

7. s_ _ _e_

8. b_o_h_ _

9. m_t_ _ _

10. f_ _h_ _

Have fun with the words!

Circle the family words!

1. pencil   (mother)   chair   purple   oval

2. heart   whiteboard   father   eraser   red

3. ruler   sister   poster   square   black

4. pink   computer   uncle   whiteout   chair

5. clock   glue   triangle   white   aunt

6. pen   blue   grandmother   star   globe

7. brother   marker   blackboard   circle   white

8. yellow   grandfather   desk   book   tape

Write the 8 words

1.	3.	5.	7.
2.	4.	6.	8.

Who is she?   Who is he?

She is my <u>mother</u>.   He is my <u>uncle</u>.

She isn't my <u>aunt</u>.   He isn't my <u>father</u>.

Write the missing words!

Who _____ he?

He is my _____.

He _____ my _____.

Who _____ _____?

She is _____ _____.

_____ isn't _____ _____.

_____ _____ he?

_____ is _____ _____.

He _____ my _____.

_____ ?

_____ .

_____ .

Is she your <u>sister</u>?   Is he your <u>brother</u>?

Yes, she is.   Yes, he is.

No, she isn't.   No, he isn't.

Write the missing words!

Is he your _____ _____?

Yes, he _____.

No, he _____.

Is _____ your _____ sister?

Yes, _____ is.

_____, she _____.

_____ he _____ _____?

Yes, _____.

No, _____.

_____ _____?

_____.

_____.

Learn the phonics

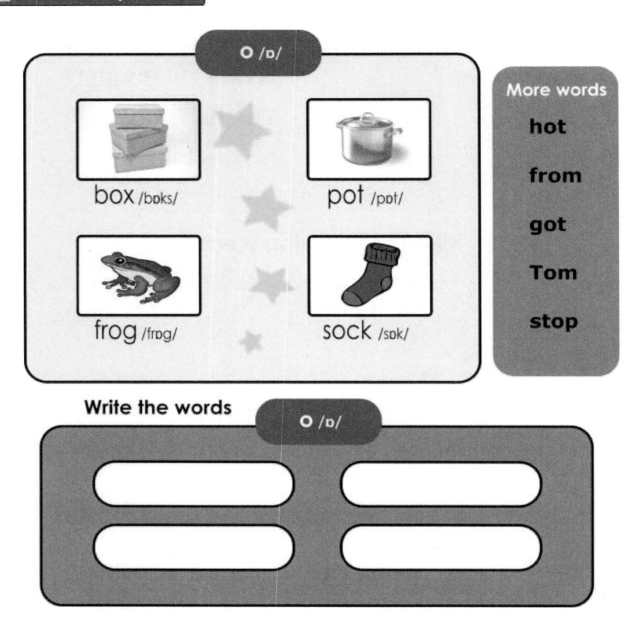

O /ɒ/

box /bɒks/

pot /pɒt/

frog /frɒg/

sock /sɒk/

More words

hot

from

got

Tom

stop

Write the words

O /ɒ/

Write the letters & Read the sentences!

The p_t is n_t h_t.

A s_ck is _n t_p _f the b_x.

T_m g_t a fr_g fr_m the sh_p.

Complete the words

1. b_____r   3. u_____e   5. f_____r

2. s_____r   4. a_____t   6. m_____r

Write the answer next to the letter "A"

A: ___ **7.** ___ is she?

a. What
b. Who
c. Whose

A: ___ **8.** ___ is my uncle.

a. She's
b. She
c. He

A: ___ **9.** Is she your sister?

a. Yes, it is.
b. Yes, she is.
c. No, she is.

A: ___ **10.** Is he ___?

a. your father
b. your aunt
c. you're brother

Answers on Page 306

Lesson 5

- Learn the words
- Learn the sentences
- Learn the phonics
- Test yourself!

Shapes

фігури

Learn the words

1. **square**
квадрат

2. **circle**
коло

3. **triangle**
трикутник

4. **oval**
овал

5. **diamond**
ромб

6. **star**
зірка

7. **rectangle**
прямокутник

8. **octagon**
восьмикутник

9. **heart**
серце

10. **pentagon**
п'ятикутник

Write the missing letters!

1. s_ _a_e

2. c_rcl_

3. tr_a_g_e

4. o_ _ _

5. d_a_o_ _

6. _t_ _

7. r_ _t_n_le

8. oc_a_o_

9. h_ _r_

10. p_n_ _ _o_

Have fun with the words!

Find the 8 shapes!

eraser   whiteboard   pentagon

oval

apple   crayon   clock   sister

book   triangle   uncle   yellow

green   whiteout

chair

pink   square

Pencil   star   grandfather   heart

desk

computer   blue   marker

diamond   mother   circle

brother   bookshelf   father

Write the 8 shapes

1.	3.	5.	7.
2.	4.	6.	8.

What is this shape?

It's a <u>square</u>.

It isn't a <u>rectangle</u>.

What are these shapes?

They're <u>octagons</u>.

They aren't <u>pentagons</u>.

Write the missing words!

What _____ this _____ ?

_____ a star.

It _____ a _____ .

What _____ these shapes?

_____ diamonds.

They aren't _____ .

What _____ this _____ ?

_____ a _____ .

_____ an _____ .

_____ ?

_____ .

_____ .

Is this a <u>triangle</u>?   Are these <u>stars</u>?

Yes, it is.   Yes, they are.

No, it isn't.   No, they aren't.

Write the missing words!

Is this an _____ ?

Yes, _____ is.

No, it _____ .

_____ these _____ ?

Yes, _____ are.

No, _____ _____ .

_____ this _____ ?

_____ , _____ is.

No, _____ .

_____ ?

_____ .

_____ .

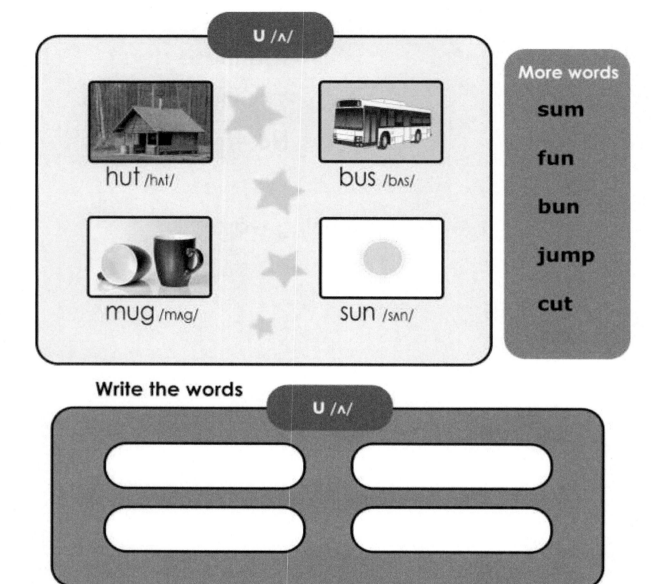

U /ʌ/

hut /hʌt/

bus /bʌs/

mug /mʌg/

sun /sʌn/

More words

sum

fun

bun

jump

cut

Write the words

U /ʌ/

Write the letters & Read the sentences!

Have f_n in the s_n.

My m_g is on the b_s.

R_n and j_mp to the h_t.

Complete the words

1. s_____r   3. o_____n   5. h_____t

2. t_____e   4. r_____e   6. d_____d

Write the answer next to the letter "A"

A: ___ **7.** What ___ shape?

a. are these
b. is this
c. is it

A: ___ **8.** ___ aren't ___.

a. It, heart
b. They're, hearts
c. They, hearts

A: ___ **9.** Is this a pentagon?

a. Yes, it is.
b. No, they aren't.
c. Yes, they are.

A: ___ **10.** ___ these ___ circles?

a. Are, shape
b. Is, a
c. Are, x

Answers on Page 306

Lesson 6

- Learn the words
- Learn the sentences
- Learn the phonics
- Test yourself!

At the zoo

в зоопарку

Learn the words

1. **monkey**
мавпа

2. **lion**
лев

3. **tiger**
тигр

4. **bear**
ведмідь

5. **rhino**
носоріг

6. **penguin**
пінгвін

7. **giraffe**
жирафа

8. **elephant**
слон

9. **crocodile**
крокодил

10. **kangaroo**
кенгуру

Write the missing letters!

1. m_n_ _y

2. l_ _ _

3. _ig_ _

4. _ _ a_

5. r_ _ _o

6. pe_g _ _n

7. gi_a_f_

8. el_ _ h_n_

9. _ro_od_ _e

10. k_n_ _r_o

Have fun with the words!

Word Search

```
e d z q f d k o v o s d j v m d y y
l f z d s o x s u o m f f x l g l y
e m k a n g a r o o o y d x k i b h
p g a o p q t n i j n u c p l r o m
h t d w e v n p a r k g g z i a e n
a u b b h b i o l p e p j v o f r j
n r p e n g u i n b y r b m v f d r
t s g c r o c o d i l e h e z e p c
m o v f a z m n f d l e t i a c r m
u i y p p v m j n e r y n i n r i m
v f i p m t i g e r x z h e d o k d
t v s k u y p a r e f w e c p v x e
```

Words are hidden → ↓ and ↘ .

kangaroo   **lion**

giraffe   **tiger**

elephant   **bear**

penguin   **crocodile**

rhino   **monkey**

Learn the sentences

What is that animal?   What are those animals?

That animal is a <u>tiger</u>.   Those animals are <u>tiger</u>s.

That animal isn't a <u>rhino</u>.   Those animals aren't <u>lion</u>s.

Write the missing words!

What _____ that _____?

_____ animal is a _____.

That animal _____ a _____.

_____ are _____ animals?

Those _____ _____ rhinos.

They aren't _____.

What _____ _____ animal?

That _____ _____ an _____.

_____ animal _____ a _____.

_____?

_____.

_____.

Is that animal a <u>giraffe</u>?   Are those <u>bears</u>?

Yes, that's a giraffe.   Yes, those are bears.

No, that isn't a giraffe.   No, those aren't bears.

Write the missing words!

Is _____ animal a _____?

Yes, _____ a penguin.

No, that _____ a _____.

_____ those tigers?

Yes, those _____ _____.

No, _____ _____ tigers.

_____ that _____ _____ _____?

_____, _____ _____ rhino.

_____, that _____ a _____.

_____ ?

_____ .

_____ .

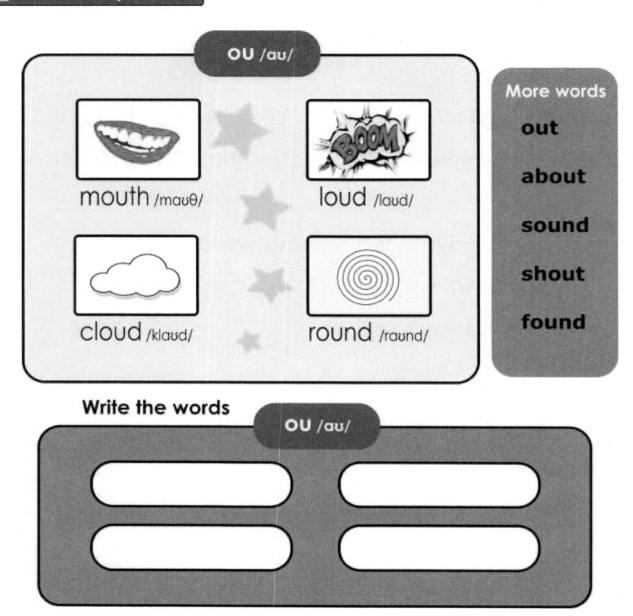

OU /aʊ/

mouth /maʊθ/

loud /laʊd/

cloud /klaʊd/

round /raʊnd/

More words

out

about

sound

shout

found

Write the words

OU /aʊ/

Write the letters & Read the sentences!

I f_ _nd a r_ _nd circle.

That is a big cl_ _d.

The lion has a l_ _d m_ _th.

Complete the words

1. s_____e   3. p_____k   5. s_____t

2. c_____a   4. r_____t   6. g_____m

Write the answer next to the letter "A"

A: ___ **7.** What ___ animals?

a. are those
b. is that
c. is this

A: ___ **8.** That ___ is a ___.

a. animals, kangaroo
b. animal, bears
c. animal, crocodile

A: ___ **9.** Are those monkeys?

a. Yes, those are monkey.
b. No, those aren't monkeys.
c. Yes, that's a monkey.

A: ___ **10.** ___ that animal a ___?

a. Are, rhinos
b. Is, rhino
c. Are, rhino

Answers on Page 306

Lesson 7
- Learn the words
- Learn the sentences
- Learn the phonics
- Test yourself!

Jobs

професії

Learn the words

1. doctor лікар	6. teacher вчитель
2. chef повар	7. farmer фермер
3. nurse медсестра	8. salesclerk продавець
4. police officer поліцейський	9. firefighter пожежник
5. taxi driver таксист	10. builder будівельник

Write the missing letters!

1. d_ _to_

2. c_e_

3. n_rs_

4. p_ _i_e of_ic_ _

5. _a_i d_i_e_

6. te_c_ _r

7. fa_ _ _r

8. s_ _e_c_e_ _

9. f_r_ _i_h_er

10. b_i_d_ _

Have fun with the words!

salesclerk
farmer
police officer
doctor
teacher

chef
builder
nurse
firefighter
taxi driver

What's his job?

He's a <u>nurse</u>.

He's not a <u>builder</u>.

What's her job?

She's a <u>doctor</u>.

She's not a <u>chef</u>.

Write the missing words!

What's _____ _____?

He's a _____.

_____ _____ a salesclerk.

_____ her _____?

_____ a _____.

She's not _____ _____.

_____ his _____?

He's a _____ driver.

_____ _____ a _____.

_____ ?

_____ .

_____ .

Is he a **police officer**?   Is she a **salesclerk**?

Yes, he is.   Yes, she is.

No, he's a **firefighter**.   No, she's a **teacher**.

Write the missing words!

Is _____ a _____ officer?

Yes, he _____ .

No, _____ a _____ .

_____ she a _____ ?

Yes, _____ _____ .

No, she's _____ taxi _____ .

_____ he _____ _____ ?

_____ , _____ _____ .

_____ , _____ a _____ .

_____ ?

_____ .

_____ .

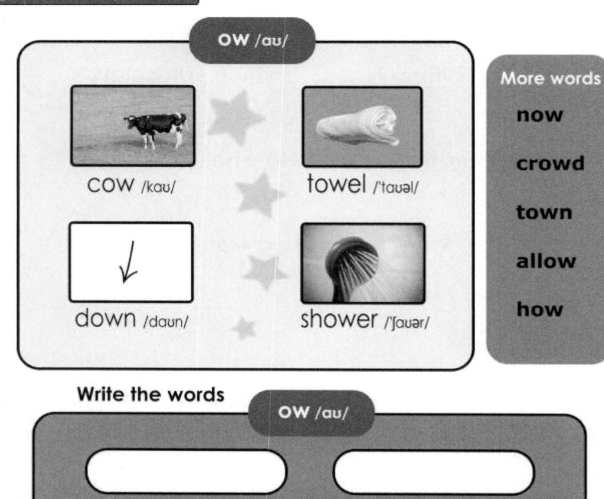

More words

now

crowd

town

allow

how

Write the words

OW /aʊ/

Write the letters & Read the sentences!

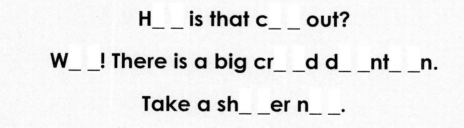

H_ _ is that c_ _ out?

W_ _! There is a big cr_ _d d_ _nt_ _n.

Take a sh_ _er n_ _.

Complete the words

1. b_____r   3. s_____k   5. t_____r

2. n_____e   4. d_____r   6. c_____f

Write the answer next to the letter "A"

A: ___ **7.** ___ his job?

a. Who's
b. What's
c. What

A: ___ **8.** She's ___ a firefighter.

a. isn't
b. is
c. not

A: ___ **9.** Is he a teacher?

a. No, she's a salesclerk.
b. No, he's a nurse.
c. No, he a doctor.

A: ___ **10.** Is she ___?

a. a farmer
b. an nurse
c. police officer

Answers on Page 306

Lesson

8

- Learn the words
- Learn the sentences
- Learn the phonics
- Test yourself!

At the fruit market

на фруктовому ринку

Learn the words

1. **apple**
   яблуко

2. **orange**
   апельсин

3. **lemon**
   лимон

4. **banana**
   банан

5. **watermelon**
   кавун

6. **pineapple**
   ананас

7. **strawberry**
   полуниця

8. **grape**
   виноград

9. **cherry**
   вишня

10. **pear**
    груша

Write the missing letters!

1. _p_l_

2. o_ _ _g_

3. l_m_ _

4. ba_ _n_

5. w_t_ _m_ _o_

6. p_n_a_ _l_

7. s_ _a_ _er_ _

8. g_a_e

9. c_e_ _y

10. p_ _ _

Have fun with the words!

Write the 3 missing words

1._____

2. _____

3. _____

apple
lemon
banana
cherry
strawberry
watermelon
pear

1._____

2. _____

3. _____

cherry
pineapple
apple
watermelon
orange
lemon
grape

1._____

2. _____

3. _____

pineapple
strawberry
orange
banana
grape
pear
cherry

1._____

2. _____

3. _____

pear
lemon
grape
apple
watermelon
banana
pineapple

1._____

2. _____

3. _____

pineapple
strawberry
orange
cherry
watermelon
grape
lemon

1._____

2. _____

3. _____

strawberry
apple
pineapple
banana
lemon
pear
orange

Which fruit do you want?   Which fruit does he want?

I want a <u>strawberry</u>.   He wants an <u>apple</u>.

I don't want a <u>lemon</u>.   He doesn't want a <u>banana</u>.

Write the missing words!

Which _____ do you _____?

I want a _____.

I _____ want a _____.

_____ fruit _____ she want?

She _____ a _____.

She _____ want an _____.

_____ fruit _____ you _____?

I _____ _____.

_____ don't _____ a _____.

_____?

_____.

_____.

Do you want a <u>grape</u>?   Does she want an <u>orange</u>?

Yes, I do.   Yes, she does.

No, I don't.   No, she doesn't.

Write the missing words!

Do _____ want a _____?

Yes, I _____.

No, _____ _____.

_____ he _____ a _____?

_____, _____ does.

No, he _____.

_____ you _____ an _____?

Yes, _____ _____.

_____, I _____.

_____?

_____.

_____.

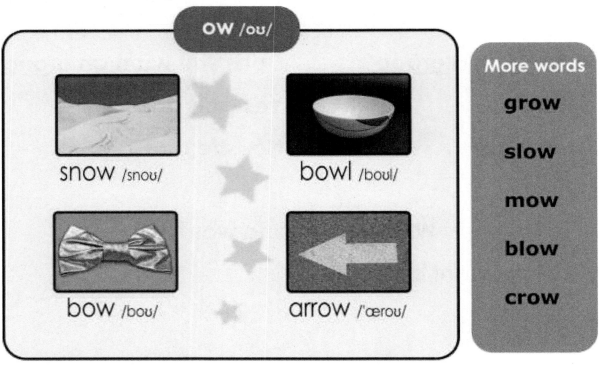

OW /ou/

snow /snou/

bowl /boul/

bow /bou/

arrow /'ærou/

More words

grow

slow

mow

blow

crow

Write the words

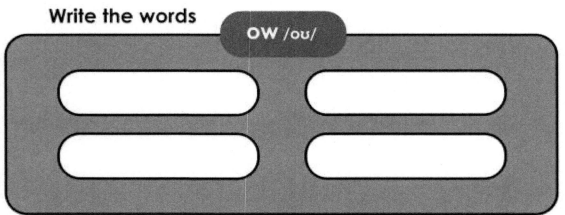

OW /ou/

Write the letters & Read the sentences!

Your yell_ _ b_ _ is in the b_ _l.

The grass gr_ _s sl_ _ly.

The black cr_ _ is in the sn_ _.

Complete the words

1. s_____y   3. w_____n   5. b_____a

2. c_____y   4. p_____e   6. l_____n

Write the answer next to the letter "A"

A: ___ **7.** Which fruit ___ she ___?

a. do, want
b. does, want
c. does, wants

A: ___ **8.** I ___ pineapple.

a. want a
b. wants a
c. want an

A: ___ **9.** Do you want a watermelon?

a. Yes, I does.
b. No, I do.
c. No, I don't.

A: ___ **10.** Does ___ want ___ orange?

a. he, a
b. you, an
c. she, an

Answers on Page 306

Lesson
9
- Learn the words
- Learn the sentences
- Learn the phonics
- Test yourself!

The body

тіло

Learn the words

1. **arm**
рука

2. **stomach**
живіт

3. **shoulder**
плече

4. **head**
голова

5. **neck**
шия

6. **toe**
палець на нозі

7. **foot**
ступня

8. **finger**
палець

9. **hand**
кисть руки

10. **leg**
нога

Write the missing letters!

1. _ _m

2. s_o_ _c_

3. _h_ _ld_r

4. _e_ _

5. n_ _ _

6. t_ _

7. _ _ _t

8. f_n_e_

9. h_ _ _

10. l_ _

Have fun with the words!

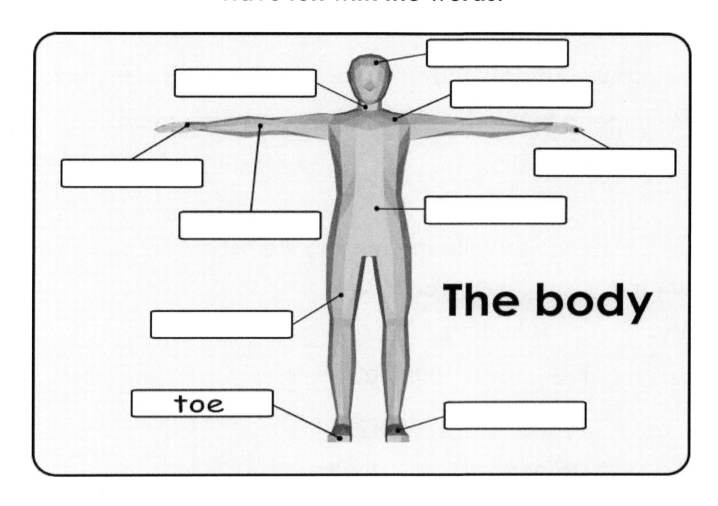

The body

toe

Unscramble the letters!

1. helosurd   _____

2. nfgire   _____

3. atohmcs   _____

4. enkc   _____

5. nhda   _____

What's wrong with <u>you</u>?   What's wrong with <u>her</u>?

My <u>finger</u> is hurting.   Her <u>arm</u> is hurting.

My <u>toe</u> isn't hurting.   Her <u>shoulder</u> isn't hurting.

Write the missing words!

What's _____ with you?

My _____ is hurting.

_____ leg _____ hurting.

_____ wrong _____ her?

_____ stomach _____ hurting.

Her _____ isn't _____.

What's _____ _____ him?

His _____ _____ _____.

_____ toe _____ _____.

_____ ?

_____ .

_____ .

Is your <u>neck</u> hurting?   Is his <u>leg</u> hurting?

Yes, my neck is hurting.   Yes, her leg is hurting.

No, my neck isn't hurting.   No, her leg isn't hurting.

Write the missing words!

Is _____ arm _____ ?

Yes, _____ arm _____ hurting.

No, my _____ isn't _____ .

_____ his _____ _____ ?

_____ , his _____ is _____ .

No, _____ hand _____ _____ .

_____ her _____ _____ ?

Yes, _____ foot _____ .

_____ , her _____ .

_____ ?

_____ .

_____ .

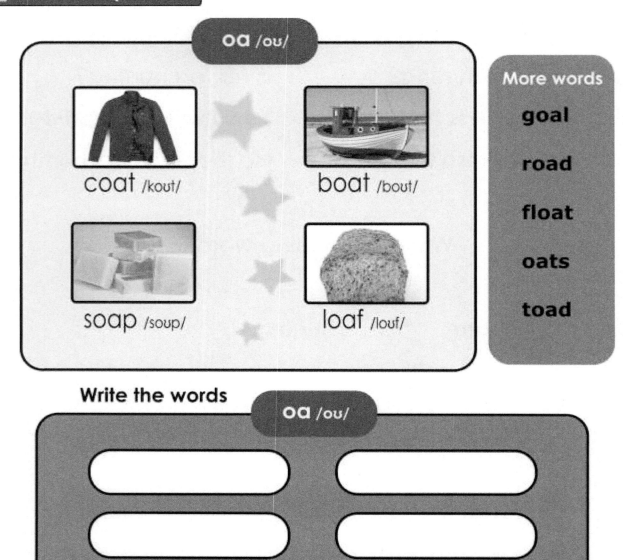

oa /ou/

coat /kout/

boat /bout/

soap /soup/

loaf /louf/

More words

goal

road

float

oats

toad

Write the words

oa /ou/

Write the letters & Read the sentences!

A t_ _d is on the r_ _d.

The s_ _p is on my c_ _t.

That b_ _t doesn't fl_ _t.

Complete the words

1. s_____h   3. f_____t   5. s_____r

2. h_____d   4. f_____r   6. n_____k

Write the answer next to the letter "A"

A: ___ **7.** What's wrong with you?

a. His toe is hurting.
b. Her toe is hurting.
c. My toe is hurting.

A: ___ **8.** His shoulder ___.

a. are hurting
b. is hurting
c. is hurt

A: ___ **9.** Is her neck hurting?

a. Yes, his neck is hurting.
b. No, her neck isn't hurting.
c. Yes, her nose is hurting.

A: ___ **10.** Is ___ leg hurting? Yes, my leg is leg hurting.

a. your
b. his
c. her

Answers on Page 306

Lesson
10
- Learn the words
- Learn the sentences
- Learn the phonics
- Test yourself!

Sports

спорт

Learn the words

1. **basketball**
баскетбол

2. **badminton**
бадмінтон

3. **golf**
гольф

4. **hockey**
хокей

5. **soccer**
футбол

6. **cricket**
крикет

7. **baseball**
бейсбол

8. **volleyball**
волейбол

9. **football**
футбол

10. **tennis**
теніс

Write the missing letters!

1. b_s_e_b_ _l

2. b_d_ _n_o_

3. g_ _ _

4. h_c_e_

5. _o_ce_

6. c_i_k_t

7. _ _s_b_l_

8. v_l_e_b_ _l

9. _o_t_ _l_

10. t_n_ _s

Have fun with the words!

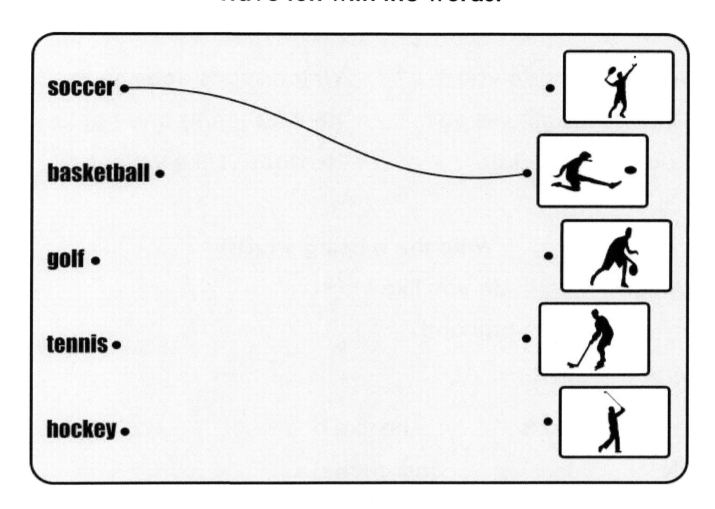

soccer •
basketball •
golf •
tennis •
hockey •

Unscramble the letters!

1. bbsaalel _____

2. lolvleaybl _____

3. lfotbalo _____

4. rctkice _____

5. nbdmtinao _____

Which sports do you like?   Which sports does he like?

I like <u>baseball</u> and <u>golf</u>.   He likes <u>tennis</u> and <u>hockey</u>.

I don't like <u>cricket</u>.   He doesn't like <u>volleyball</u>.

Write the missing words!

Which _____ do you like?

I _____ baseball and _____.

I _____ like _____.

_____ sports _____ he like?

He _____ _____ and cricket.

He _____ _____.

Which _____ does _____ _____?

_____ likes football _____ _____.

She _____ _____.

_____?

_____.

_____.

Do you like <u>badminton</u>?   Does she like <u>tennis</u>?

Yes, I do.   Yes, she does.

No, I don't.   No, she doesn't.

Write the missing words!

Do you _____ _____ ?

Yes, _____ _____ .

No, _____ _____ .

_____ he _____ _____ ?

_____ , he _____ .

No, _____ _____ .

_____ she _____ ?

Yes, _____ _____ .

_____ , _____ doesn't.

_____ ?

_____ .

_____ .

Learn the phonics

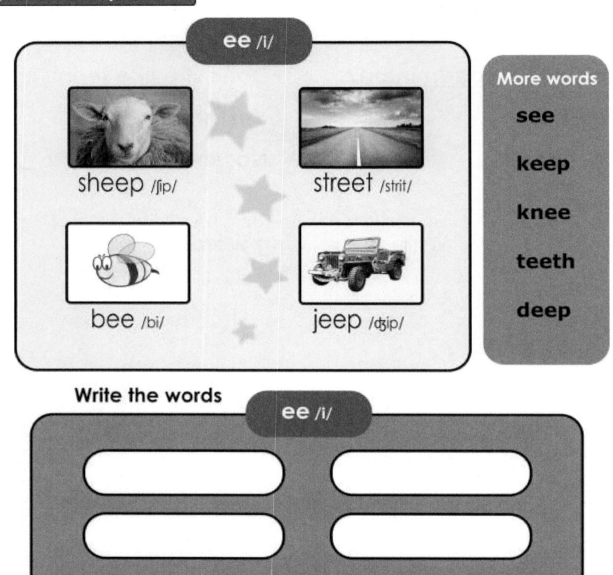

ee /i/

sheep /ʃip/

street /strit/

bee /bi/

jeep /dʒip/

More words

see

keep

knee

teeth

deep

Write the words

ee /i/

Write the letters & Read the sentences!

I s_ _ a j_ _p on the str_ _t.

A b_ _ is on the sh_ _p's kn_ _.

She k_ _ps her t_ _th clean.

Complete the words

1. t_____s   3. g_____f   5. b_____n

2. v_____l   4. c_____t   6. h_____y

Write the answer next to the letter "A"

A: ___ **7.** Which sports ___ you like?

a. do
b. does
c. is

A: ___ **8.** He ___ volleyball.

a. don't like
b. doesn't likes
c. doesn't like

A: ___ **9.** Does she like badminton?

a. Yes, she does.
b. No, he doesn't.
c. No, she does.

A: ___ **10.** ___ you like tennis?

a. Does
b. Do
c. Are

Answers on Page 306

Lesson 11
- Learn the words
- Learn the sentences
- Learn the phonics
- Test yourself!

Places

місця

Learn the words

1. **store**
магазин

2. **swimming pool**
басейн

3. **department store**
універмаг

4. **supermarket**
супермаркет

5. **night market**
нічний ринок

6. **cinema**
кінотеатр

7. **beach**
пляж

8. **park**
парк

9. **gym**
спортзал

10. **restaurant**
ресторан

Write the missing letters!

1. s _ o _ _

2. sw _ m _ i _ g p _ _ l

3. d _ p _ _ t _ e _ t s _ o _ e

4. su _ _ r _ a _ k _ _

5. n _ _ _ t m _ r _ e _

6. c _ n _ _ _ _

7. b _ a _ _

8. p _ _ _

9. g _ _

10. r _ s _ a _ r _ _ t

- 66 -

Have fun with the words!

Word Search

```
k u w t n v a h l g d r w t y n n a
w u w d c s w i m m i n g p o o l g
n i g h t m a r k e t m r b k y z z
l s u p e r m a r k e t y p l r t m
l l n l i x o d w r u d y y a m n s
u g s b a o z b x a w c p a z r x h
a u f e d y q k m h l p z g y m k m
d e p a r t m e n t s t o r e t q d
s n t c z y c i n e m a g r a c p q
c z f h p o s t o r e v d n s i z i
v u p l u r o t y u c y e p w r b o
v v b a r e s t a u r a n t b e c c
```

Word directions: ➡ ↘ ⬇

beach	**park**
cinema	**restaurant**
department store	**store**
gym	**supermarket**
night market	**swimming pool**

JOE'S PIZZA

Where do you want to go?   Where does he want to go?

I want to go to the <u>beach</u>.   He wants to go to the <u>store</u>.

I don't want to go to the <u>gym</u>.   He doesn't want to go to the <u>gym</u>.

Write the missing words!

Where _____ you want _____ go?

I want to _____ to the _____ .

I _____ want to go _____ the department _____ .

_____ does _____ want to _____ ?

He _____ to go _____ the _____ pool.

He _____ want _____ go to the _____ .

Where _____ you _____ to _____ ?

I _____ to _____ the _____ .

I _____ _____ to _____ to the _____ .

_____ ?

_____ .

_____ .

Do you want to go to the <u>park</u>?   Does she want to go to the <u>cinema</u>?

Yes, I do.   Yes, she does.

No, I don't want to.   No, she doesn't want to.

Write the missing words!

Do you _____ to _____ to the _____ pool?

Yes, _____ _____.

No, I _____ _____ to.

_____ he _____ to go _____ the _____?

_____, he _____.

No, he _____ want _____.

_____ you _____ to go to _____ _____?

Yes, _____ _____.

_____, I _____ _____ _____.

_____?

_____.

_____.

ea /i/

beach /bitʃ/   read /rid/

leaf /lif/   bean /bin/

More words

jeans

cheap

team

wheat

clean

Write the words

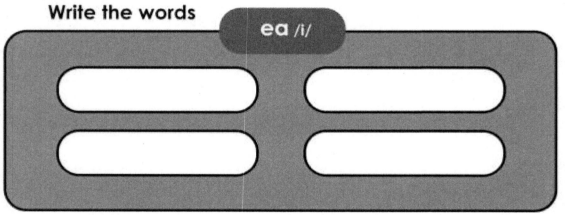

ea /i/

Write the letters & Read the sentences!

These j_ _ns are r_ _lly ch_ _p.

A b_ _n is on the green l_ _f.

Pl_ _se cl_ _n the b_ _ch.

Complete the words

1. s_____e   3. p_____k   5. s_____t

2. c_____a   4. r_____t   6. g_____m

Write the answer next to the letter "A"

A: ___ **7.** Where ___ he want to go?

a. do
b. does
c. is

A: ___ **8.** I ___ go to the night market.

a. want
b. want to
c. wants to

A: ___ **9.** Does she want to go to the park?

a. No, she don't want to.
b. No, she does.
c. No, she doesn't want to.

A: ___ **10.** Do you want to ___ the swimming pool?

a. go to
b. go
c. goes to

Answers on Page 306

Lesson 12

- Learn the words
- Learn the sentences
- Learn the phonics
- Test yourself!

Clothes

одяг

Learn the words

1. **T-shirt**
футболка

2. **blouse**
блузка

3. **dress**
плаття

4. **coat**
пальто

5. **scarf**
шарф

6. **hat**
капелюх

7. **sweater**
светр

8. **necktie**
краватка

9. **skirt**
спідниця

10. **jacket**
куртка

Write the missing letters!

1. T-_ _ir_

2. b_o_s_

3. d_e_s_

4. c_ _t

5. s_ar_

6. h_ _

7. s_ea_e_

8. _e_kt_e

9. s_i_t

10. ja_k_t

Have fun with the words!

T-shirt
blouse
dress
coat
scarf

n e c k t i e

hat
sweater
necktie
skirt
jacket

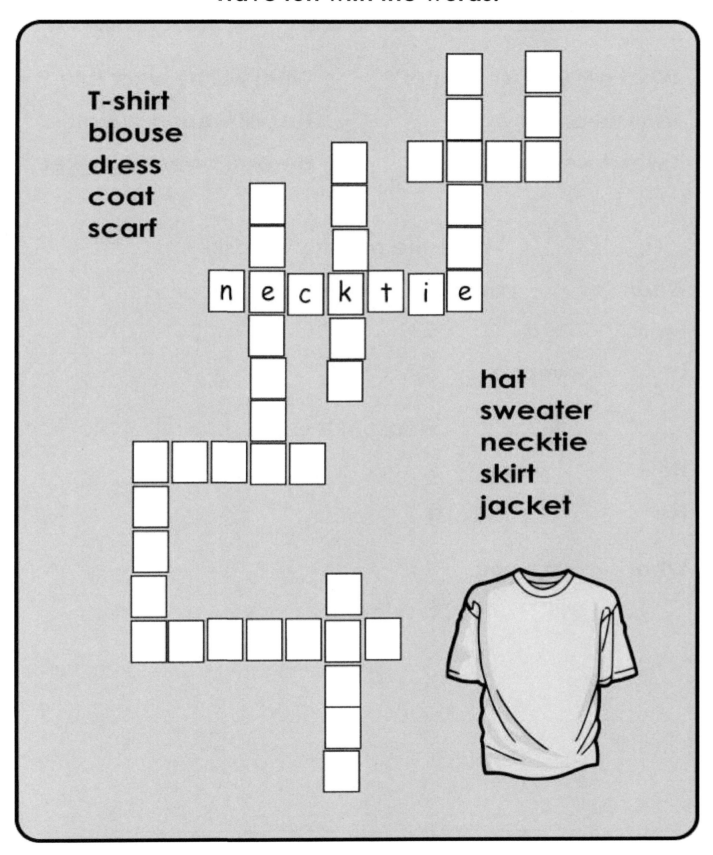

What will you wear later?   What will he wear later?

I will wear a <u>dress</u>.   He will wear a <u>sweater</u>.

I won't wear a <u>skirt</u>.   He won't wear a <u>jacket</u>.

Write the missing words!

What _____ you _____ later?

I will _____ a _____ .

I _____ wear a _____ .

_____ will _____ wear _____ ?

He _____ wear _____ _____ .

He _____ _____ a _____ .

What _____ you _____ _____ ?

_____ will _____ a skirt.

I _____ _____ a _____ .

_____ ?

_____ .

_____ .

Will you wear a <u>necktie</u> later?   Will she wear a <u>T-shirt</u> later?

Yes, I will.   Yes, she will.

No, I won't.   No, she won't.

Write the missing words!

Will you _____ a _____ later?

Yes, I _____.

No, _____.

_____ he _____ a _____ _____?

_____, he _____.

No, _____ _____.

_____ you _____?

_____, _____ will.

_____, _____.

_____?

_____.

_____.

Learn the phonics

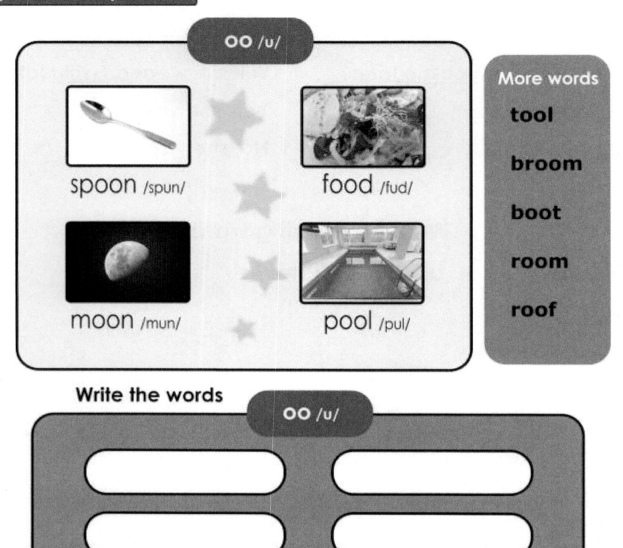

OO /u/

spoon /spun/

food /fud/

moon /mun/

pool /pul/

More words

tool

broom

boot

room

roof

Write the words

OO /u/

Write the letters & Read the sentences!

Eat your f_ _d with a sp_ _n.

There's a p_ _l in that r_ _m.

Use these t_ _ls to fix the r_ _f.

Complete the words

1. b_____e   3. n_____e   5. s_____f

2. s_____r   4. j_____t   6. d_____s

Write the answer next to the letter "A"

A: ___ **7.** What ___ he wear later?

a. do
b. will
c. does

A: ___ **8.** He ___ a coat.

a. won't wears
b. won't wear
c. will wears

A: ___ **9.** Will she wear a skirt later?

a. No, she won't.
b. No, she willn't.
c. No, she will.

A: ___ **10.** Will you wear ___ later?

a. a necktie
b. dress
c. hats

Answers on Page 306

Lesson
13
- Learn the words
- Learn the sentences
- Learn the phonics
- Test yourself!

School subjects

шкільні предмети

Learn the words

1. **English**
англійська

2. **computer**
інформатика

3. **social studies**
соціологія

4. **geography**
географія

5. **physical education (P.E.)**
фізична культура

6. **art**
образотворче мистецтво

7. **math**
математика

8. **science**
природничі науки

9. **history**
історія

10. **music**
музика

Write the missing letters!

1. E_g_i_h

2. c_m_ut_r

3. so_ _a_ s_ud_e_

4. g_o_r_p_y

5. p_y_i_al e_u_a_ _on

6. a_ _

7. m_ _ _

8. s_i_ _ce

9. hi_t_ _ _

10. _us_c

Have fun with the words!

Write the 3 missing words

1._____

2. _____

3. _____

math

English

science

physical education

history

social studies

computer

1._____

2. _____

3. _____

history

music

physical education

art

math

geography

science

1._____

2. _____

3. _____

English

math

social studies

geography

computer

art

music

1._____

2. _____

3. _____

math

art

physical education

music

science

geography

social studies

1._____

2. _____

3. _____

history

social studies

music

art

English

computer

math

1._____

2. _____

3. _____

science

history

physical education

art

computer

English

geography

Learn the sentences

What class do you have today?

Today, I have <u>geography</u> class.

I don't have <u>music</u> class.

What class does he have today?

Today, he has <u>English</u> class.

He doesn't have <u>math</u> class.

Write the missing words!

What _____ do you _____ today?

_____, I have _____ class.

I _____ have _____ education _____.

_____ class _____ she have _____?

Today, she _____ _____ class.

_____ _____ have _____ studies class.

What class _____ you _____ _____?

Today, _____ have _____ _____.

I _____ _____ math _____.

_____ ?

_____ .

_____ .

Do you have <u>history</u> class today?   Does she have <u>art</u> class today?

Yes, I do.   Yes, she does.

No, I don't.   No, she doesn't.

Write the missing words!

Do you _____ social _____ class _____?

Yes, I _____.

No, _____.

_____ he _____ _____ class _____?

_____, he _____.

No, _____ _____.

_____ you _____ physical _____ _____ today?

_____, _____ do.

_____, I _____.

_____?

_____.

_____.

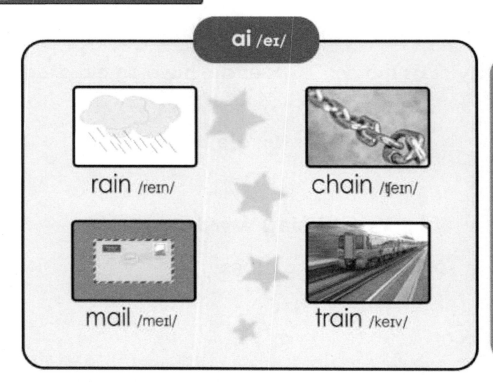

ai /eɪ/

rain /reɪn/ chain /ʧeɪn/

mail /meɪl/ train /keɪv/

More words

aim

wait

pain

rail

tail

Write the words

ai /eɪ/

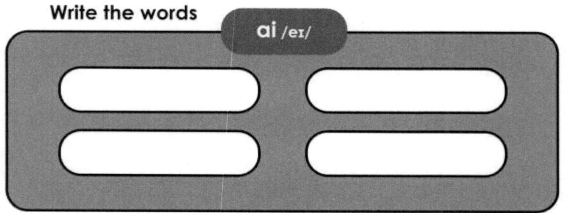

Write the letters & Read the sentences!

The sn_ _l is in the r_ _n ag_ _n.

I w_ _t for the tr_ _n.

There is b_ _t by the s_ _l.

Complete the words

1. g _____ y   3. h _____ y   5. E _____ h

2. c _____ r   4. m _____ c   6. s _____ e

Write the answer next to the letter "A"

A: ___ **7.** What class ___ today?

a. does she have
b. does you have
c. does he has

A: ___ **8.** Today, he ___ social studies class.

a. have
b. has
c. haves

A: ___ **9.** Do you have physical education class today?

a. Yes, I have.
b. Yes, I do.
c. Yes, I does.

A: ___ **10.** ___ she ___ math class today?

a. Does, has
b. Do, have
c. Does, have

Answers on Page 306

Lesson
14
- Learn the words
- Learn the sentences
- Learn the phonics
- Test yourself!

Vegetables

овочі

Learn the words

1. **potato**
картопля

2. **carrot**
морква

3. **pumpkin**
гарбуз

4. **broccoli**
брокколі

5. **asparagus**
спаржа

6. **cabbage**
капуста

7. **spinach**
шпинат

8. **corn**
кукурудза

9. **onion**
цибуля

10. **mushroom**
гриб

Write the missing letters!

1. p_t_t_

2. c_ _r_ _

3. _u_p_ _n

4. b_o _ _ol_

5. _s_a_ _g_s

6. c_b_a_e

7. s_i_a_ _

8. _o_ _

9. _n_o_

10. m_s_ _o_ _

Have fun with the words!

Circle the vegetable words!

1. golf   (carrot)   art   park   stomach

2. beach   asparagus   neck   eraser   lemon

3. history   tennis   pumpkin   leg   gym

4. grape   computer   onion   hockey   music

5. spinach   hat   apple   store   foot

6. pen   head   badminton   skirt   corn

7. blouse   potato   arm   circle   pear

8. orange   jacket   desk   cabbage   finger

Write the 8 words

1. _____
2. _____
3. _____
4. _____
5. _____
6. _____
7. _____
8. _____

Learn the sentences

What did you eat for dinner?   What did they eat for dinner?

We ate <u>corn</u> for dinner.   They ate <u>broccoli</u> for dinner.

We didn't eat <u>mushroom</u>.   They didn't eat <u>asparagus</u>.

Write the missing words!

What _____ you _____ for dinner?

We _____ spinach for _____ .

We _____ eat _____ .

What _____ they _____ for _____ ?

They _____ _____ for _____ .

_____ didn't _____ _____ .

What _____ you _____ _____ _____ ?

I _____ _____ _____ _____ .

_____ _____ eat _____ for _____ .

_____ ?

_____ .

_____ .

Did you eat <u>broccoli</u> for dinner? Did they eat <u>potato</u> for dinner?

Yes, we did. Yes, they did.

No, we didn't. We ate <u>cabbage</u>. No, they didn't. They ate <u>onion</u>.

Write the missing words!

Did you _____ asparagus _____ dinner?

Yes, we _____ .

No, _____ didn't. We _____ _____ .

_____ they eat _____ for _____ ?

_____ , they _____ .

No, _____ _____ . They ate _____ .

Did you _____ _____ _____ dinner?

Yes, _____ _____ .

_____ , we _____ . We _____ _____ .

_____ ?

_____ .

_____ .

Learn the phonics

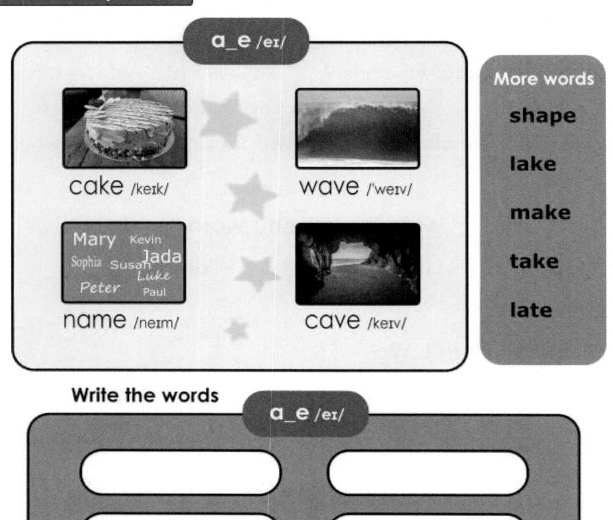

a_e /eɪ/

cake /keɪk/

wave /ˈweɪv/

name /neɪm/

cave /keɪv/

More words

shape

lake

make

take

late

Write the words

a_e /eɪ/

Write the letters & Read the sentences!

His n_m_ is the s_m_ as mine.

There is a c_v_ near the l_k_.

You can t_k_ the c_k_ home.

Complete the words

1. c_____t

3. b_____i

5. m_____m

2. p_____o

4. s_____h

6. o_____n

Write the answer next to the letter "A"

A: ___ **7.** What did you eat ___ dinner?

a. of
b. for
c. on

A: ___ **8.** They ___ pumpkin.

a. didn't ate
b. didn't eaten
c. didn't eat

A: ___ **9.** Did you eat spinach for dinner?

a. No, we didn't. We ate potato.
b. No, we didn't. We eat cabbage.
c. No, we did. We ate corn.

A: ___ **10.** Did they ___ mushroom for dinner?

a. ate
b. eats
c. eat

Answers on Page 306

Lesson 15

- Learn the words
- Learn the sentences
- Learn the phonics
- Test yourself!

At the toy shop

у магазині іграшок

Learn the words

1. **car**
машинка

2. **airplane**
Літак

3. **dinosaur**
динозавр

4. **doll**
лялька

5. **teddy bear**
плюшевий ведмедик

6. **jump rope**
скакалка

7. **board game**
настільна гра

8. **toy block**
конструктор

9. **robot**
робот

10. **ball**
м'яч

Write the missing letters!

1. c_ _

2. a_r_la_e

3. d_n_sa_r

4. do_ _

5. t_d_y b_a_

6. ju_p r_p_

7. b_a_d ga_e

8. t_y b_oc_s

9. r_bo_

10. _al_

Have fun with the words!

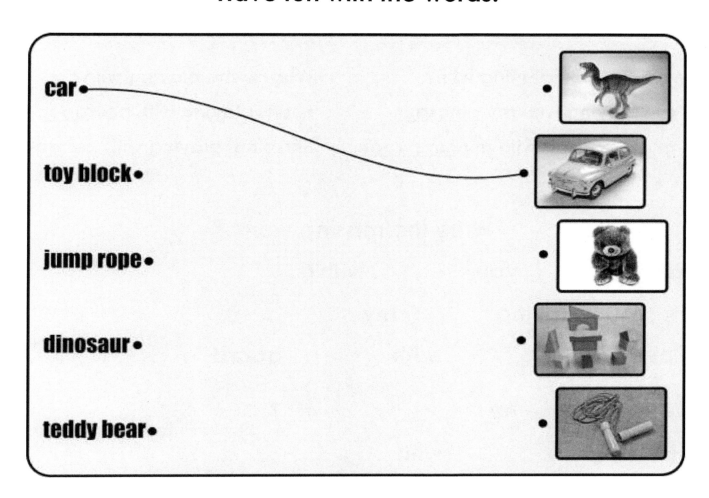

Unscramble the letters!

1. analirpe _____

2. oldl _____

3. robad agem _____

4. albl _____

5. broto _____

What are you playing with?   What is she playing with?

I am playing with my <u>dinosaur</u>.   She is playing with her <u>robot</u>.

I'm not playing with my <u>jump rope</u>.   She's not playing with her <u>doll</u>.

Write the missing words!

What _____ you _____ with?

I _____ playing _____ my _____ .

I'm _____ _____ with _____ board _____ .

What _____ he _____ _____ ?

He _____ _____ with _____ _____ .

_____ not _____ _____ his _____ .

_____ is _____ playing _____ ?

She _____ with _____ _____ jump _____ .

_____ playing _____ her _____ .

_____ ?

_____ .

_____ .

Are you playing with your <u>car</u>?   Is he playing with his <u>ball</u>?

Yes, I am.   Yes, he is.

No, I'm playing with my <u>doll</u>.   No, he's playing with his <u>robot</u>.

Write the missing words!

Are you _____ with _____ _____?

Yes, I _____.

No, _____ playing _____ my _____.

_____ she _____ _____ her _____ blocks?

_____, _____ is.

No, _____ _____ with _____ _____ bear.

Is _____ with _____ _____?

_____, he _____.

_____, _____ _____ his _____.

_____?

_____.

_____.

i_e /aɪ/

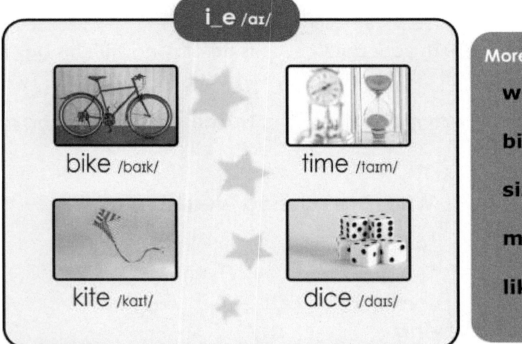

bike /baɪk/

time /taɪm/

kite /kaɪt/

dice /daɪs/

More words

white

bite

size

mine

like

Write the words

i_e /aɪ/

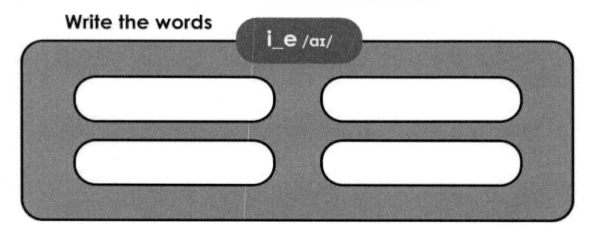

Write the letters & Read the sentences!

The wh_t_ b_k_ is m_n_.

I l_k_ this k_t_.

The small s_z_ is f_n_.

Complete the words

1. a_____e   3. r_____t   5. b_____l

2. d_____r   4. t_____r 6. d_____l

Write the answer next to the letter "A"

A: ___ **7.** What ___ she playing ___?

a. are, with
b. is, of
c. is, with

A: ___ **8.** He is ___ teddy bear.

a. play with his
b. playing with his
c. playing with her

A: ___ **9.** Are you playing with your jump rope?

a. No, I'm playing with my dinosaur.
b. No, I playing with my toy blocks.
c. Yes, I are.

A: ___ **10.** ___ playing with ___ doll?

a. Is you, your
b. Is she, her
c. Are she, her

Answers on Page 306

Lesson
16
- Learn the words
- Learn the sentences
- Learn the phonics
- Test yourself!

In the kitchen

на кухні а

Learn the words

1. **refrigerator**
холодильник

2. **cupboard**
шафа

3. **microwave oven**
мікрохвильова піч

4. **dish rack**
стійка для посуду

5. **coffee maker**
кавоварка

6. **toaster**
тостер

7. **stove**
піч

8. **pan**
tava

9. **rice cooker**
рисоварка

10. **blender**
блендер

Write the missing letters!

1. _ef_i_era_or

2. c_p_o_ _d

3. m_c_ow_ _e o_ _n

4. d_s_ ra_ _

5. _o_f_e m_k_ _

6. to_s_e_

7. _to_ _

8. p_ _

9. r_c_ c_ok_ _

10. _l_nd_r

Have fun with the words!

Find the 8 kitchen items!

banana hockey crocodile

doctor foot teacher

refrigerator tennis

ball pan robot

yellow

lion head elephant

giraffe math blender Pencil

baseball

monkey arm eraser

cupboard computer stove

square star rice cooker

circle

dish rack toaster father

Write the 8 shapes

1.	3.	5.	7.
2.	4.	6.	8.

What does your kitchen need?

Our kitchen needs a new <u>stove</u>.

It doesn't need a <u>rice cooker</u>.

Write the missing words!

What _____ your _____ need?

_____ kitchen _____ a _____ _____.

It _____ _____ a _____ rack.

What _____ _____ kitchen _____?

Their _____ needs _____ _____ _____.

_____ doesn't _____ a microwave _____.

_____ does _____ _____ _____?

Our _____ _____ _____ new _____.

_____ need _____ _____.

_____ ?

_____ .

_____ .

Does their kitchen need a new <u>refrigerator</u>?

Yes, their kitchen does.

No, it doesn't need a new one.

Write the missing words!

Does _____ kitchen _____ a new _____ ?

_____ , our _____ does.

No, _____ need a _____ _____ .

Does their _____ need a _____ _____ maker?

Yes, _____ kitchen _____ .

_____ , it doesn't _____ _____ one.

_____ your _____ a _____ _____ ?

_____ , _____ _____ does.

No, _____ new _____ .

_____ ?

_____ .

_____ .

Learn the phonics

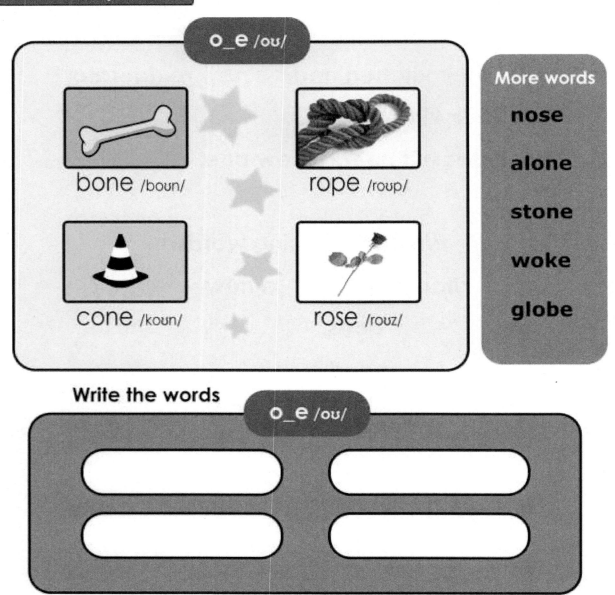

o_e /ou/

bone /boun/	rope /roup/
cone /koun/	rose /rouz/

More words

nose

alone

stone

woke

globe

Write the words

o_e /ou/

Write the letters & Read the sentences!

A r_s_ is on the st_n_.

The dog smells the b_n_ with its n_s_.

He r_d_ his bike al_n_.

- 100 -

Complete the words

1. b_____r   3. p_____n   5. c_____d

2. s_____e   4. t_____r   6. r_____r

Write the answer next to the letter "A"

A: ___ **7.** What ___ your kitchen ___?

a. does, need
b. does, needs
c. do, need

A: ___ **8.** It ___ need a microwave oven.

a. does'nt
b. doesn't
c. don't

A: ___ **9.** Does your kitchen need a new dish rack?

a. Yes, our kitchen does.
b. No, it does need a new one.
c. Yes, their kitchen does.

A: ___ **10.** ___ kitchen need a new stove?

a. Does they're
b. Does there
c. Does their

Answers on Page 306

Lesson
17

- Learn the words
- Learn the sentences
- Learn the phonics
- Test yourself!

Feelings

почуття

Learn the words

1. **fine**
   в порядку

2. **sad**
   сумний

3. **bored**
   знуджений

4. **energetic**
   енергійний

5. **tired**
   втомлений

6. **angry**
   сердитий

7. **happy**
   щасливий

8. **excited**
   збуджений

9. **frustrated**
   розчарований

10. **sick**
    хворий

Write the missing letters!

1. _in_

2. _a_

3. _o_ _d

4. e_er_et_ _

5. t_r_ _

6. a_g_ _

7. _a_ _y

8. _xci_e_

9. f_u_t_a_ _d

10. s_c_

Have fun with the words!

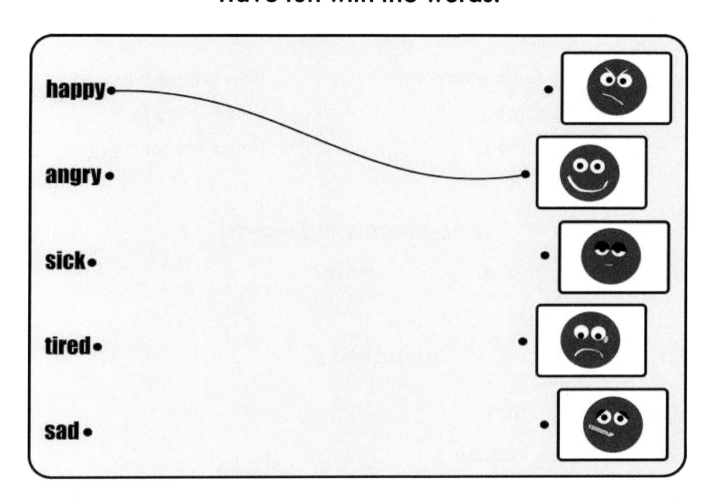

Unscramble the letters!

1. nregetiec _____

2. rdufsrtaet _____

3. dbreo _____

4. xectdei _____

5. inef _____

How are you feeling now?	How is he feeling now?
I'm feeling <u>energetic</u>.	He's feeling <u>fine</u>.
I'm not feeling <u>tired</u>.	He isn't feeling <u>angry</u>.

Write the missing words!

How _____ you _____ now?

_____ feeling _____ .

I'm _____ _____ energetic.

How _____ he _____ _____ ?

He's _____ happy.

_____ _____ feeling _____ .

_____ are _____ feeling _____ ?

I'm _____ _____ .

_____ _____ _____ frustrated.

_____?

_____.

_____.

Are you feeling <u>frustrated</u> now?   Is she feeling <u>bored</u> now?

Yes, I am.   Yes, she is.

No, I'm feeling <u>happy</u>.   No, she's feeling <u>excited</u>.

Write the missing words!

Are _____ feeling _____ now?

Yes, I _____.

No, _____ feeling _____.

_____ she _____ tired _____?

_____, she _____.

No, she's _____ _____.

_____ you _____ _____ _____?

Yes, _____ _____.

_____, I'm _____ _____.

_____?

_____.

_____.

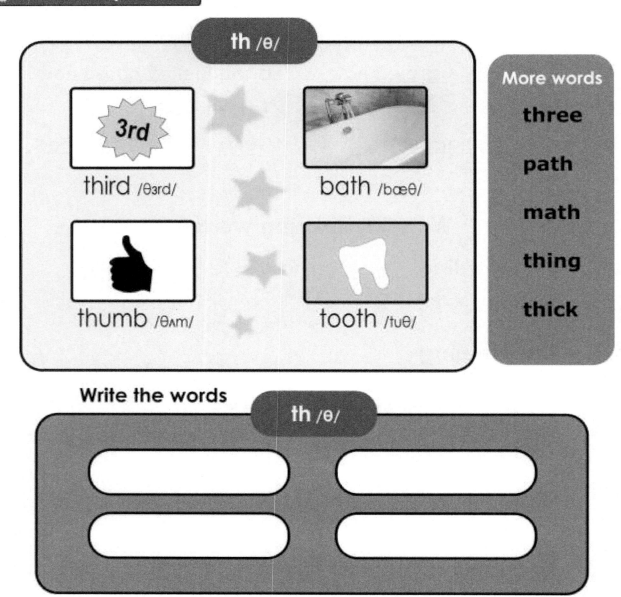

th /θ/

3rd
third /θɜrd/

bath /bæθ/

thumb /θʌm/

tooth /tuθ/

More words

three

path

math

thing

thick

Write the words

th /θ/

Write the letters & Read the sentences!

He put his _ _umb in the ba_ _.

He has _ _ree _ _ick ma_ _ books.

The _ _ird pa_ _ is wide.

Complete the words

1. a_____y   3. b_____d   5. e_____c

2. s_____d   4. t_____d   6. f_____d

Write the answer next to the letter "A"

A: ___ **7.** How is he ___?

a. feeling
b. feels
c. felt

A: ___ **8.** How ___ you feeling?

a. is
b. am
c. are

A: ___ **9.** He ___ feeling frustrated.

a. isn't
b. aren't
c. not

A: ___ **10.** Are you feeling tired?

a. Yes, I'm not.
b. Yes, I am.
c. No, I isn't.

Answers on Page 306

- Learn the words
- Learn the sentences
- Learn the phonics
- Test yourself!

At the ice cream shop

в кафе-морозиві

Learn the words

1. **mint**
м'ята

2. **cherry**
вишня

3. **strawberry**
полуниця

4. **chocolate**
шоколад

5. **raspberry**
малина

6. **almond**
мигдаль

7. **coconut**
кокос

8. **coffee**
кава

9. **vanilla**
ваніль

10. **caramel**
карамель

Write the missing letters!

1. m_ _ _

2. _h_ _r_

3. st_a_b_ _r_

4. c_o_o_ _t_

5. r_ _p_ _r_y

6. a_ _o_ _

7. c_ _o_u_

8. _o_ _e_

9. v_ _i_ _a

10. ca_ _m_ _

Have fun with the words!

Word Search

```
z  c  s  w  q  p  n  r  v  c  h  e  r  r  y  w  g  n
r  o  w  c  s  c  z  q  a  g  z  e  y  m  u  e  a  w
c  f  x  n  h  t  a  j  l  s  s  j  q  u  i  l  d  s
f  f  c  f  d  o  r  r  d  f  p  a  n  q  p  n  w  m
r  e  o  v  w  z  c  a  a  w  a  b  m  h  y  m  t  d
k  e  c  s  a  c  i  o  w  m  q  l  e  q  r  m  x  u
k  u  o  p  a  n  t  r  l  b  e  r  m  r  x  y  p  y
r  b  n  q  t  h  i  x  y  a  e  l  d  o  r  b  r  e
f  g  u  e  n  h  p  l  w  y  t  r  d  m  n  y  g  y
l  i  t  z  n  k  c  f  l  l  u  e  r  h  a  d  y  w
l  v  u  s  d  k  q  d  j  a  o  r  r  y  s  w  d  l
g  h  m  n  v  b  m  l  m  j  q  u  d  q  y  u  m  n
```

Word directions:

mint	almond
cherry	coconut
strawberry	coffee
chocolate	vanilla
raspberry	caramel

What's your favorite ice cream flavor?

My favorite ice cream flavor is <u>chocolate</u>.

My favorite ice cream flavor isn't <u>strawberry</u>.

Write the missing words!

What's _____ favorite _____ cream flavor?

My _____ ice _____ flavor is _____ .

_____ favorite ice cream _____ _____ vanilla.

_____ his _____ ice cream _____ ?

His _____ ice _____ flavor _____ _____ .

_____ favorite _____ cream _____ isn't _____ .

_____ favorite _____ cream _____ ?

Her _____ ice _____ _____ _____ .

_____ favorite _____ _____ flavor isn't _____ .

_____ ?

_____ .

_____ .

Do you like <u>mint</u> flavor?

Yes, mint flavor is my favorite.

No, I don't like mint flavor.

Does he like <u>cherry</u> flavor?

Yes, cherry flavor is my favorite.

No, he doesn't like cherry flavor.

Write the missing words!

Do you _____ raspberry _____?

Yes, _____ flavor is my _____.

_____, I _____ like raspberry _____.

_____ she like _____ flavor?

_____, almond flavor is _____ favorite.

No, she _____ like _____ flavor.

Does he like coffee flavor?

_____, coffee _____ is _____ favorite.

No, _____ doesn't _____ _____ flavor.

_____ ?

_____ .

_____ .

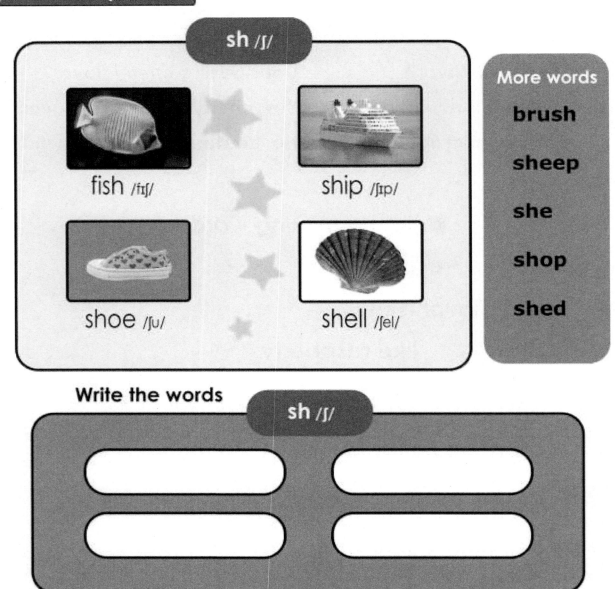

sh /ʃ/

fish /fɪʃ/

ship /ʃɪp/

shoe /ʃu/

shell /ʃel/

More words

brush

sheep

she

shop

shed

Write the words

sh /ʃ/

Write the letters & Read the sentences!

_ _e is bru_ _ing her teeth.

That _ _op has cheap _ _oes.

The _ _eep is in the _ _ed.

Complete the words

1. s_____y   3. c_____e   5. c_____y

2. r_____y   4. v_____a   6. a_____d

Write the answer next to the letter "A"

A: ___ **7.** What's your favorite ice cream flavor?

a. My favorite ice cream is chocolate.
b. His favorite ice cream flavor is mint.
c. My favorite ice cream flavor is cherry.

A: ___ **8.** My favorite ice cream flavor ___ caramel.

a. aren't
b. isn't
c. is'nt

A: ___ **9.** Does she like cherry flavor?

a. Yes, cherry flavor is his favorite.
b. No, she doesn't likes cherry flavor.
c. No, she doesn't like cherry flavor.

A: ___ **10.** Do you like mint flavor? Yes, mint flavor ___ favorite.

a. is my
b. is her
c. is his

Answers on Page 306

Lesson 19
- Learn the words
- Learn the sentences
- Learn the phonics
- Test yourself!

The weather

погода

Learn the words

1. sunny сонячна	**6. cold** холодна
2. rainy дощова	**7. warm** тепла
3. snowy сніжна	**8. hot** жарка
4. cloudy марна	**9. freezing** крижана, морозна
5. windy вітряна	**10. cool** прохолодна

Write the missing letters!

1. s_n_ _   6. c_ _d

2. _a_n_   7. w_ _ _

3. s_ _ _y   8. h_ _

4. c_o_d_   9. f_e_ _in_

5. w_n_ _   10. _ _ o _

Have fun with the words!

sunny
rainy
snowy
cloudy
windy
cold
warm
hot
freezing
cool

f r e e z i n g

Write the missing word:

How's the weather going to be?

The weather is going to be <u>sunny</u>.

The weather isn't going to be <u>rainy</u>.

Write the missing words!

How's the _____ going _____ be?

The weather _____ _____ to _____ _____.

_____ weather _____ going _____ be _____.

_____ the _____ _____ to _____ ?

_____ is _____ to be _____.

The _____ isn't _____ _____ _____.

_____ weather _____ _____ be?

_____ going to _____.

The _____ _____ to _____.

_____ ?

_____.

_____.

Is the weather going to be <u>hot</u>?

Yes, it's going to be hot.

No, it's not going to be hot.

Write the missing words!

Is _____ weather _____ to _____ _____?

Yes, _____ going _____ _____ cloudy.

_____, it's _____ _____ to be _____.

_____ the _____ going _____ _____ cool?

Yes, _____ _____ _____ be _____.

No, _____ not _____ _____ be _____.

Is _____ _____ going _____ be _____?

Yes, _____ _____ to _____ _____.

_____, it's _____ _____ _____ windy.

_____?

_____.

_____.

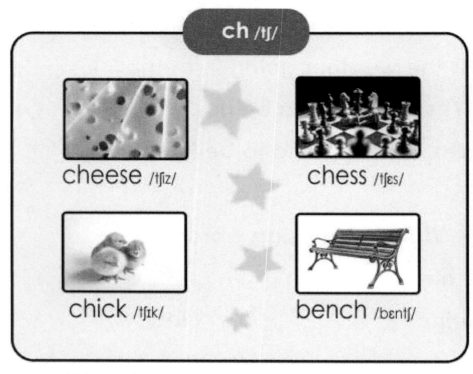

More words

check

chin

cheap

chat

choose

Write the words

ch /tʃ/

Write the letters & Read the sentences!

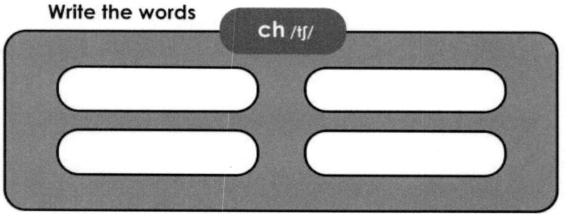

There is _ _eese on your _ _in.

We sit on the ben_ _ and _ _at.

I will _ _oose the _ _eap _ _air.

Complete the words

1. c _____ y   3. f _____ g   5. w _____ m

2. s _____ y   4. r _____ y   6. c _____ d

Write the answer next to the letter "A"

A: ___ **7.** How's the weather going to be?

a. It's going be freezing.
b. It not going to be cold.
c. It's going to be warm.

A: ___ **8.** It's not ___ be windy.

a. going to
b. go to
c. going too

A: ___ **9.** Is the weather going to be cloudy?

a. No, it not going to be cloudy.
b. Yes, it's going be cloudy.
c. Yes, it's going to be cloudy.

A: ___ **10.** Is ___ going to be hot?

a. weather
b. this weather
c. the weather

Answers on Page 306

Lesson 20

- Learn the words
- Learn the sentences
- Learn the phonics
- Test yourself!

In the living room

в вітальні

Learn the words

1. **coffee table**
журнальний столик

2. **armchair**
крісло

3. **clock**
годинник

4. **television**
телевізор

5. **bookcase**
книжкова шафа

6. **sofa**
диван

7. **vase**
ваза

8. **rug**
килим

9. **TV stand**
підставка під телевізор

10. **painting**
картина

Write the missing letters!

1. _of_ _e t _ _ l_

2. a_ _c_a_r

3. c_ _c_

4. te_e_ _si_n

5. b_ _k_a_e

6. s_ _ _

7. v_ _ _

8. _u_

9. T_ s_a_ _

10. _a_ _t_n_

Have fun with the words!

1. table / front / the / is / of / in / coffee

The sofa _____.

2. to / stand / TV / next / the / is

The vase _____.

3. next / the / painting / to / is

The clock _____.

4. the / in / of / sofa / front / isn't

The bookcase _____.

5. of / the / in / rug / front / isn't

The painting _____.

6. isn't / TV / the / stand / to / next

The armchair _____.

7. in / table / of / coffee / the / is / front

The television _____.

8. next / the / isn't / vase / to

The rug _____.

Where is the <u>coffee table</u>?

The coffee table is in front of the <u>TV stand</u>.

It isn't next to the <u>sofa</u>.

Write the missing words!

Where _____ the _____ stand?

The TV _____ is _____ to the _____ .

It _____ in front _____ the _____ .

_____ is _____ _____ table?

The coffee _____ is in _____ of the _____ .

It _____ next _____ _____ _____ .

Where _____ _____ _____ ?

The painting _____ _____ to _____ _____ .

It _____ in _____ the _____ .

_____?

_____.

_____.

Is the <u>sofa</u> next to the <u>armchair</u>?

Yes, the sofa is.

No, the sofa isn't.

Write the missing words!

Is the _____ table _____ to _____ _____ ?

Yes, _____ coffee _____ _____ .

_____ , the _____ _____ isn't.

_____ the painting in _____ of the _____ ?

Yes, _____ is.

No, _____ painting _____ .

Is _____ TV _____ next _____ the _____ ?

Yes, _____ _____ stand _____ .

_____ , _____ TV _____ _____ .

_____ ?

_____ .

_____ .

Learn the phonics

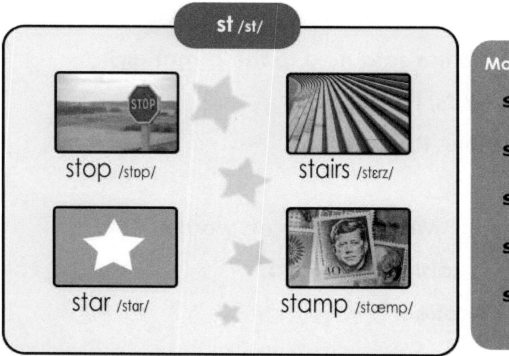

st /st/

stop /stɒp/

stairs /stɛrz/

star /star/

stamp /stæmp/

More words

stool

store

storm

sting

stove

Write the words

st /st/

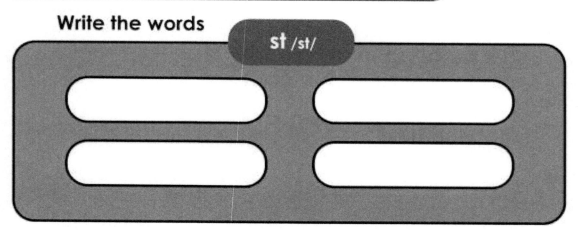

Write the letters & Read the sentences!

There is a _ _ar on this _ _amp.

_ _op at this _ _ore and buy a new _ _ove.

Put a _ _ool in front of the _ _airs.

Complete the words

1. c_____k   3. b_____e   5. t_____n

2. a_____r   4. s_____a   6. p_____g

Write the answer next to the letter "A"

A: ___ **7.** Where is the clock?

a. The clock is next of the bookcase.
b. The clock is next to the bookcase.
c. The clock is front of the bookcase.

A: ___ **8.** The vase is in ___ the sofa.

a. front to
b. next to
c. front of

A: ___ **9.** Is the television next to the coffee table?

a. Yes, the coffee table is.
b. Yes, television is.
c. No, the television isn't.

A: ___ **10.** Is ___ in front of the rug?

a. the armchair
b. these armchair
c. armchair

Answers on Page 306

Lesson 21
- Learn the words
- Learn the sentences
- Learn the phonics
- Test yourself!

Chores

хатня робота

Learn the words

1. **take out the trash**
виносити сміття

2. **wash the dishes**
мити посуд

3. **feed the pets**
годувати домашніх тварин

4. **vacuum the carpet**
пилососити килим

5. **clean the bedroom**
прибирати в спальні

6. **iron the clothes**
прасувати одяг

7. **mop the floor**
мити підлогу

8. **cook dinner**
готувати обід

9. **do the laundry**
прати

10. **make the beds**
заправляти постіль

Write the missing letters!

1. ta_e o_t th_ t_a_h

2. w_ _h t_e di_h_s

3. _ _ed _he pe_ _

4. v_cu_m t_e c_r_e_

5. cl_ _n th_ b_ _r_om

6. i_o_ t_e c_ot_e_

7. m_p _he f_oo_

8. c_o_ d_n_e_

9. d_ t_e l_u_d_y

10. m_ _e _he b_ _s

Have fun with the words!

do	the beds
clean	the laundry
make	the floor
iron	the bedroom
mop	dinner
cook	the dishes
take out	the clothes
wash	the trash

Write the 2 missing chores!

1. _____

2. _____

Which chores do you have to do?

_____

Which chores do you have to do today?

Today, I have to <u>wash the dishes</u>.

I don't have to <u>clean the bedroom</u> today.

Write the missing words!

Which _____ do you _____ to _____ today?

Today, I have _____ take _____ the _____ .

I _____ have to _____ the dishes _____ .

Which chores _____ he have _____ do today?

_____ , he has _____ feed the _____ .

He doesn't _____ to _____ the clothes today.

_____ chores does _____ have _____ do _____ ?

Today, she _____ to do _____ _____ .

She _____ have _____ _____ dinner _____ .

_____ ?

_____ .

_____ .

Do you have to <u>mop the floor</u> today?

Yes, I have to mop the floor.

No, I have to <u>take out the trash</u>.

Write the missing words!

Do you _____ to _____ the carpet _____?

Yes, _____ have _____ vacuum the _____.

_____, I _____ to _____ _____ pets.

Does _____ have _____ clean the _____ today?

_____, she has to _____ _____ bedroom.

No, _____ to _____ the clothes.

_____ he _____ to _____ the beds _____?

Yes, _____ has _____ make _____ _____.

_____, he _____ to _____ _____ dishes.

_____?

_____.

_____.

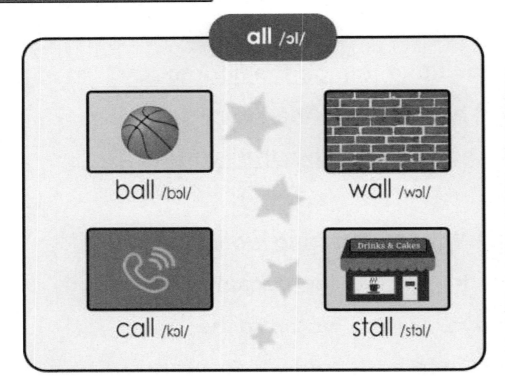

all /ɔl/

ball /bɔl/

wall /wɔl/

call /kɔl/

stall /stɔl/

More words

all

small

mall

tall

fall

Write the words

all /ɔl/

Write the letters & Read the sentences!

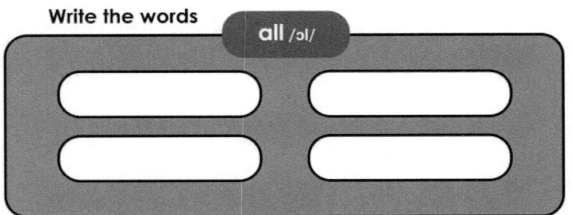

This b_ _ _ is too sm_ _ _.

There is a st_ _ _ in the m_ _ _.

The t_ _ _ man will c_ _ _ you.

Complete the words

1. l_____y   3. c_____s   5. b_____m

2. c_____t   4. f_____r   6. d_____r

Write the answer next to the letter "A"

A: ___ **7.** Which chores ___ you have to ___ today?

a. do, do
b. does
c. is

A: ___ **8.** She ___ make the beds. She ___ to mop the floor.

a. has to, doesn't has
b. have to, doesn't have
c. has to, doesn't have

A: ___ **9.** Does he have to vacuum the carpet today?

a. Yes, he have to vacuum the carpet.
b. No, he has to vacuum the dishes.
c. No, he has to do the laundry.

A: ___ **10.** Does ___ have to feed the pets today?

a. you
b. she
c. they

Answers on Page 306

Lesson 22
- Learn the words
- Learn the sentences
- Learn the phonics
- Test yourself!

Pets

домашні тварини

Learn the words

1. **rabbit**
   кролик

2. **cat**
   кіт

3. **dog**
   собака

4. **guinea pig**
   морська свинка

5. **bird**
   пташка

6. **fish**
   рибка

7. **turtle**
   черепаха

8. **mouse**
   мишка

9. **hamster**
   хом'як

10. **snake**
    змія

Write the missing letters!

1. r_ _b_t

2. _a_

3. d_ _

4. g_i_e_ p_ _

5. b_ _d

6. f_s_

7. t_r_l_

8. m_u_e

9. ha_s_ _r

10. s_ _ke

Have fun with the words!

r
r a
a b
b b
i
t

hamster
snake
mouse
cat
guinea pig
dog
turtle
fish
rabbit
bird

Write the missing word:

Which pet would you like to get?

I would like to get a <u>hamster</u>.

I wouldn't like to get a <u>snake</u>.

Write the missing words!

Which _____ would you _____ to get?

I _____ like to _____ a _____ .

I wouldn't _____ _____ get _____ fish.

Which pet _____ she like _____ _____ ?

_____ would _____ to _____ a turtle.

She _____ like _____ _____ a _____ .

_____ _____ would they _____ to _____ ?

They _____ like _____ get _____ _____ pig.

_____ wouldn't _____ to _____ a _____ .

_____ ?

_____ .

_____ .

Would you like to get a <u>dog</u>?

Yes, I would like to get a dog.

No, I would like to get a <u>cat</u>.

Write the missing words!

Would you _____ to get _____ fish?

Yes, I _____ like to get a _____ .

No, _____ would _____ to _____ a _____ .

Would they _____ to get a _____ ?

Yes, _____ would like _____ get _____ rabbit.

_____ , they _____ _____ to get a _____ .

Would _____ like _____ get a _____ ?

_____ , he would like _____ _____ a _____ .

No, he _____ _____ get _____ bird.

_____ ?

_____ .

_____ .

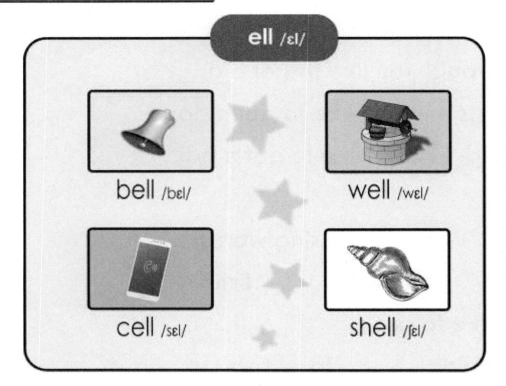

ell /ɛl/

bell /bɛl/

well /wɛl/

cell /sɛl/

shell /ʃɛl/

More words

tell

smell

fell

yell

sell

Write the words

ell /ɛl/

Write the letters & Read the sentences!

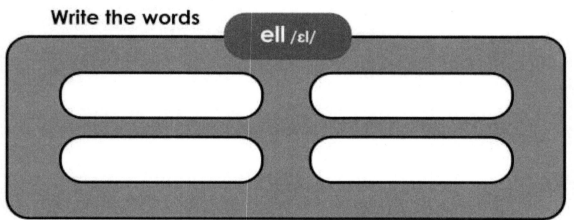

This sh_ _ _ sm_ _ _s like the beach.

T_ _ _ me why he is y_ _ _ing.

The b_ _ _ f_ _ _ down the w_ _ _.

Complete the words

1. r_____t   3. s_____e   5. t_____e

2. h_____r   4. m_____e   6. b_____d

Write the answer next to the letter "A"

A: ___ **7.** Which pet would you like to get?

a. I would like to get a turtle.
b. I will like to get a hamster.
c. I will like a cat.

A: ___ **8.** She would like ___ a mouse. She ___ like to get a snake.

a. get, wouldnt'
b. to get, wouldn't
c. to get, would'nt

A: ___ **9.** Would he like to get a guinea pig?

a. No, he would like to get a guinea pig.
b. No, he wouldn't like to get a rabbit.
c. No, he would like to get a rabbit.

A: ___ **10.** Would she ___ a fish?

a. likes to get
b. like get to
c. like to get

Answers on Page 306

Lesson
23

- Learn the words
- Learn the sentences
- Learn the phonics
- Test yourself!

Skills

навички

Learn the words

1. **swim**
   плавати

2. **ski**
   кататися на лижах

3. **sing**
   співати

4. **draw**
   малювати

5. **read**
   читати

6. **cook**
   готувати

7. **surf**
   займатися серфінгом

8. **ride**
   їхати

9. **write**
   писати

10. **run**
    бігати

Write the missing letters!

1. s_i_

2. _k_

3. si_ _

4. d_ _w

5. r_ _d

6. _o_k

7. s_ _f

8. r_d_

9. _ri_e

10. r_ _

Have fun with the words!

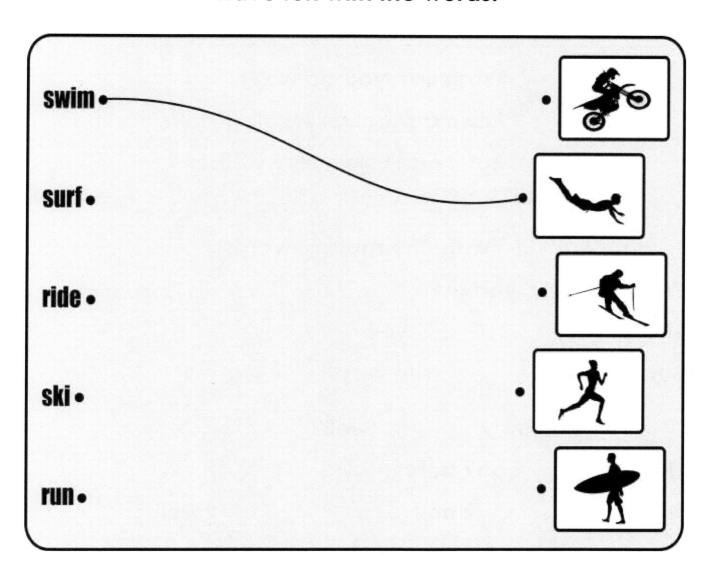

Write 4 more skills!

1. _____   3. _____

2. _____   4. _____

What can you do well?

_____

What can you do well?

I can <u>dance</u> very well.

But, I can't <u>sing</u> very well.

Write the missing words!

What _____ you do _____?

I can _____ _____ well.

But, _____ _____ run very _____.

_____ can they _____ well?

They _____ cook very _____.

_____, _____ can't _____ _____ well.

What _____ _____ do _____?

He _____ _____ _____ _____.

_____, he _____ _____ very _____.

_____ _____ _____ _____ _____?

_____ _____ _____ _____ _____.

_____ _____ _____ _____ _____.

Can you <u>surf</u> well?

Yes, I can surf very well.

No, but I can <u>ski</u> very well.

Write the missing words!

Can _____ write _____ ?

Yes, _____ can _____ very _____ .

No, _____ I _____ read _____ well.

_____ she _____ well?

_____ , she can draw _____ well.

No, _____ can _____ very _____ .

_____ you _____ _____ ?

Yes, we _____ swim _____ well.

_____ , but _____ can _____ very _____ .

_____ ?

_____ .

_____ .

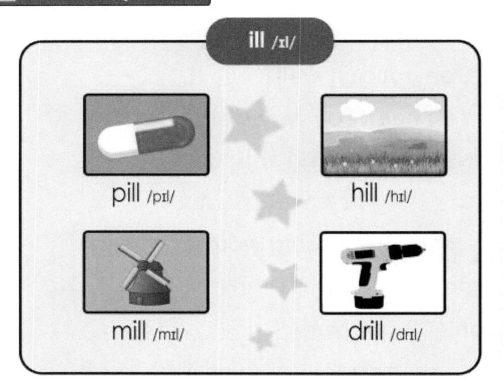

ill /ɪl/

pill /pɪl/

hill /hɪl/

mill /mɪl/

drill /drɪl/

More words

will

still

fill

grill

spill

Write the words

ill /ɪl/

Write the letters & Read the sentences!

The beef is st_ _ _ on the gr_ _ _.

There is a m_ _ _ on the h_ _ _.

I w_ _ _ use my dr_ _ _ to fix the m_ _ _.

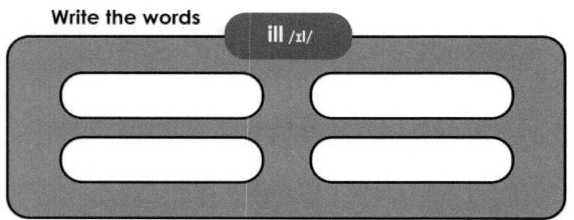

Complete the words

1. s _____ m   3. r _____ d   5. w _____ e

2. s _____ g   4. c _____ k   6. d _____ w

Write the answer next to the letter "A"

A: ___ **7.** What can you do ___?

a. goodly
b. good
c. well

A: ___ **8.** He ___ very well. But, he ___ very well.

a. can swims, can't surfs
b. can swim, can't surf
c. can swim, can surf

A: ___ **9.** Can she write well?

a. Yes, she can write very well.
b. Yes, she can writes very well.
c. No, but she can read very good.

A: ___ **10.** Can he ___ well?

a. sings
b. draw
c. wrote

Answers on Page 306

Lesson 24

- Learn the words
- Learn the sentences
- Learn the phonics
- Test yourself!

Meats

м'ясо

Learn the words

1. **beef**
   яловичина

2. **fish**
   риба

3. **pork**
   свинина

4. **salami**
   салямі

5. **bacon**
   бекон

6. **chicken**
   курятина

7. **sausage**
   ковбаса

8. **lamb**
   баранина

9. **shrimp**
   креветки

10. **ham**
    шинка

Write the missing letters!

1. b_ _f

2. _i_h

3. _o_k

4. s_l_ _i

5. b_ _ _n

6. c_ _c_en

7. s_ _sa_e

8. l_m_

9. _h_i_p

10. h_ _

Have fun with the words!

Word Search

```
c d u y f t r r l p i f b a p s a e
x m z o r b t w q f u e w a q o x k
m e c h i c k e n a y r r o j x r s
b m b s s k u u i r l j o u s b c k
x a a l a x u s q h a r g r c i r q
x e c m u f x n a q m j z z s x p j
w b o t s p l v b l b j a y h a m y
o w n q a q n h y e a x d m r r n o
g g l l g c x g d n e m n d i k y z
p a e o e a v v v c c f i k m h y k
d x f h h h r f i s h b d p p p z o
l p h x q v y t n n p f f t x h p g
```

Word directions: ➡ ↘ ⬇

beef	**chicken**
fish	**sausage**
pork	**lamb**
salami	**shrimp**
bacon	**ham**

What will you be cooking for lunch?

I will be cooking <u>chicken</u> for lunch.

I won't be cooking <u>beef</u>.

Write the missing words!

What _____ you be _____ for _____?

I will _____ cooking pork _____ lunch.

_____ _____ be cooking _____.

_____ will he _____ _____ for lunch?

He _____ be cooking _____ for _____.

_____ won't _____ _____ bacon.

What will _____ _____ cooking _____ _____?

She _____ be _____ shrimp _____ lunch.

She _____ _____ cooking _____.

_____?

_____.

_____.

Will you be cooking <u>fish</u> for lunch?

Yes, I will be.

No, I won't be. I'll be cooking <u>sausage</u>.

Write the missing words!

Will you _____ cooking ham _____ lunch?

Yes, _____ will _____ .

No, I _____ be. _____ be cooking _____ .

_____ she be _____ _____ for _____ ?

Yes, she _____ _____ .

No, _____ won't be. She'll _____ _____ salami.

Will _____ _____ cooking _____ _____ lunch?

_____ , he _____ .

_____ , he _____ be. _____ be _____ _____ .

_____ ?

_____ .

_____ .

Learn the phonics

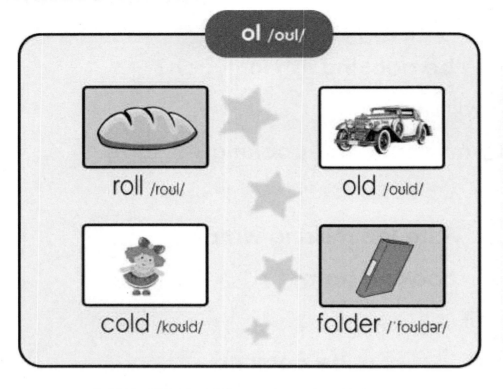

ol /oul/

roll /roul/

old /ould/

cold /kould/

folder /ˈfouldər/

More words

scroll

sold

told

mold

bold

Write the words

ol /oul/

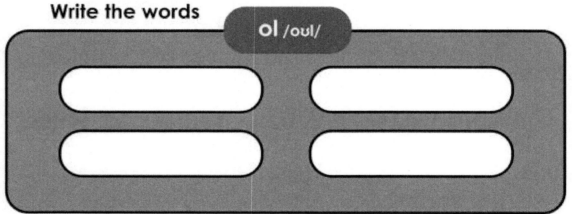

Write the letters & Read the sentences!

My father s_ _d the _ _d car.

There is m_ _d on the r_ _l.

I put the scr_ _l in the f_ _der.

Complete the words

1. b____f   3. s____i   5. b____n

2. c____n   4. s____p   6. s____e

Write the answer next to the letter "A"

A: ___ **7.** What will he be eating ___ lunch?

a. for
b. of
c. on

A: ___ **8.** I ___ eating fish for lunch.

a. will been
b. will be
c. won't

A: ___ **9.** Will she be eating beef for lunch?

a. No, she won't be. She'll be eat pork.
b. No, she won't. She'll be eating pork.
c. No, she won't be. She'll be eating pork.

A: ___ **10.** Will they ___ ham for lunch?

a. be eat
b. eating
c. be eating

Answers on Page 306

Lesson 25

- Learn the words
- Learn the sentences
- Learn the phonics
- Test yourself!

Countries

країни

Learn the words

1. **Canada**
Канада

2. **Brazil**
Бразилія

3. **Japan**
Японія

4. **Australia**
Австралія

5. **South Africa**
Південна Африка

6. **Mexico**
Мексика

7. **Germany**
Німеччина

8. **China**
Китай

9. **Russia**
Росія

10. **England**
Англія

Write the missing letters!

1. C_ _a_a

2. B_a_ _l

3. _ap_n

4. A_st_a_ _a

5. S_u_h Af_i_ _

6. _ex_c_

7. G_r_a_y

8. C_i_ _

9. R_ _si_

10. _n_la_d

Have fun with the words!

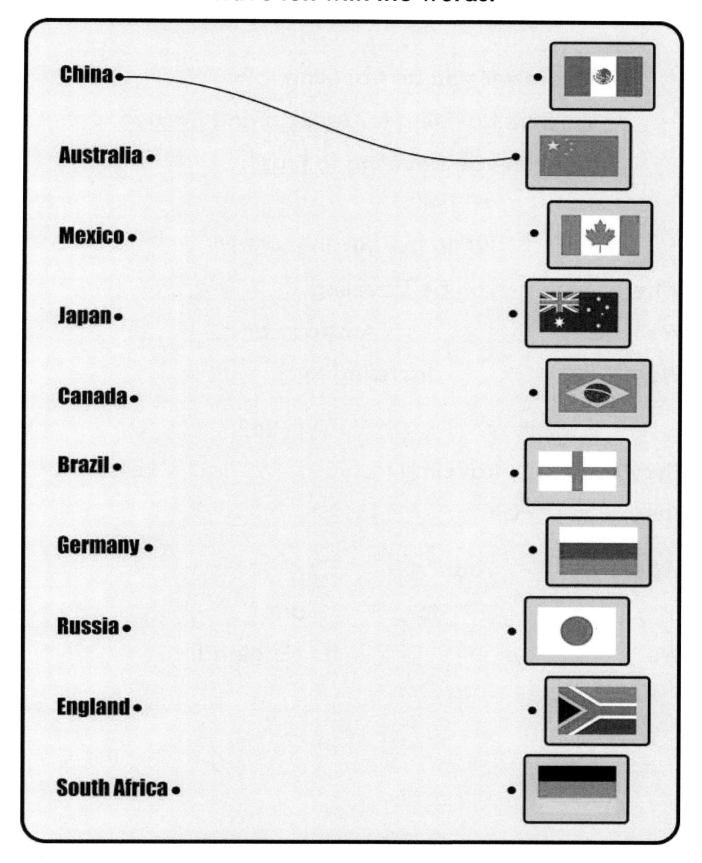

Where will you be traveling to?

We'll be traveling to <u>Canada</u> and <u>Mexico</u>.

We won't be traveling to <u>Brazil</u>.

Write the missing words!

Where _____ you be traveling _____?

We'll be _____ _____ Australia and _____.

We _____ traveling to _____.

_____ will they _____ _____ to?

They'll _____ traveling to _____ _____ Russia.

They _____ be _____ to _____.

Where _____ you _____ _____ _____?

_____ be _____ to _____ and _____.

We _____ be _____ _____ England.

_____?

_____.

_____.

Will they be traveling to <u>China</u>?

Yes, they will be.

No, they won't be. They'll be traveling to <u>Japan</u>.

Write the missing words!

Will they _____ traveling _____ South _____?

Yes, _____ will _____.

No, _____ won't be. They'll be _____ to _____.

_____ you be _____ to Russia?

Yes, we _____ _____.

No, _____ won't be. We'll _____ traveling to _____.

Will _____ be traveling to _____?

_____, they _____ _____.

No, they _____ be. _____ be _____ to _____.

_____ ?

_____ .

_____ .

ar /ar/

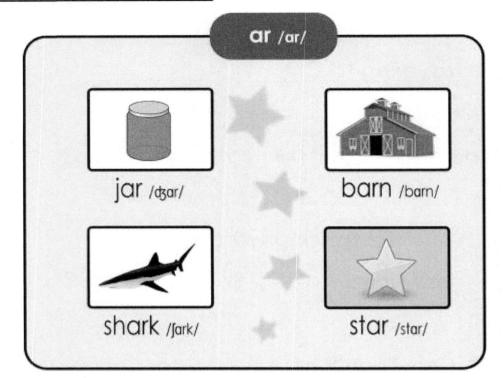

jar /dʒar/

barn /barn/

shark /ʃark/

star /star/

More words

dark

park

farm

car

arm

Write the words

ar /ar/

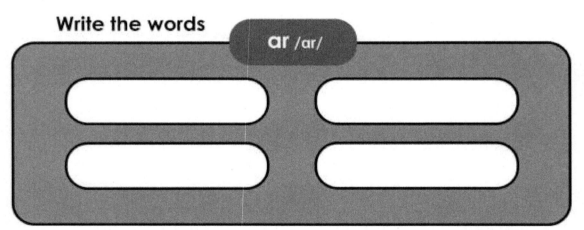

Write the letters & Read the sentences!

There is a b_ _n on the f_ _m.

That st_ _ is f_ _.

I hurt my _ _m at the p_ _k.

Complete the words

1. A_____ a   3. M_____ o   5. J_____ n

2. G_____ y   4. E_____ d   6. R_____ a

Write the answer next to the letter "A"

A: ___ **7.** Where will you ___ to?

a. be travel
b. be traveling
c. been traveling

A: ___ **8.** ___ traveling to Mexico and Brazil.

a. They'll
b. They're be
c. They'll be

A: ___ **9.** Will you be traveling to Canada?

a. No, we won't be. We'll be traveling to England.
b. No, we won't. We'll be travel to England.
c. No, we wont'. We'll be traveling to England.

A: ___ **10.** Will they be ___ Japan?

a. traveling
b. traveling to
c. travel to

Answers on Page 306

Lesson
26
- Learn the words
- Learn the sentences
- Learn the phonics
- Test yourself!

Languages

мови

Learn the words

1. **English**
англійська

2. **German**
німецька

3. **Portuguese**
португальська

4. **Japanese**
японська

5. **Vietnamese**
в'єтнамська

6. **Spanish**
іспанська

7. **French**
французька

8. **Chinese**
китайська

9. **Hindi**
хінді

10. **Arabic**
арабська

Write the missing letters!

1. E_g_i_h

2. _er_a_

3. P_ _tu_u_se

4. _ap_n_se

5. Vi_t_ _me_e

6. S_a_i_h

7. F_en_ _

8. _h_ne_e

9. H_n_ _

10. A_a_i_

Have fun with the words!

➢ **Write the words in your language!**

Vietnamese	_____
German	_____
Japanese	_____
Spanish	_____
English	_____
Arabic	_____
Hindi	_____
Portuguese	_____
Chinese	_____
French	_____

Unscramble the letters!

1. HECNISE _____

2. HSASNIP _____

3. IATEVNEMES _____

4. EAPNEJAS _____

5. GORETUPUES _____

What language do people speak in <u>Germany</u>?

They speak German in Germany.

They don't speak <u>Spanish</u> in Germany.

Write the missing words!

What _____ do _____ speak _____ Vietnam?

They speak _____ in _____ .

They _____ speak _____ in Vietnam.

What language _____ people _____ _____ Mexico?

_____ speak Spanish _____ Mexico.

They don't _____ _____ in _____ .

_____ language _____ people _____ in _____ ?

_____ speak _____ _____ Japan.

They _____ speak _____ in _____ .

_____ ?

_____ .

_____ .

Do people speak <u>English</u> in <u>Australia</u>?

Yes, they do.

Nobody speaks <u>French</u> in Australia.

Write the missing words!

Do people _____ Portuguese _____ Brazil?

_____ , they _____ .

Nobody speaks _____ in _____ .

Do _____ speak _____ in China?

Yes, _____ _____ .

_____ _____ Hindi _____ China.

_____ people speak _____ in _____ ?

_____ , _____ do.

Nobody _____ _____ England.

_____ _____ ?

_____ _____ .

_____ _____ .

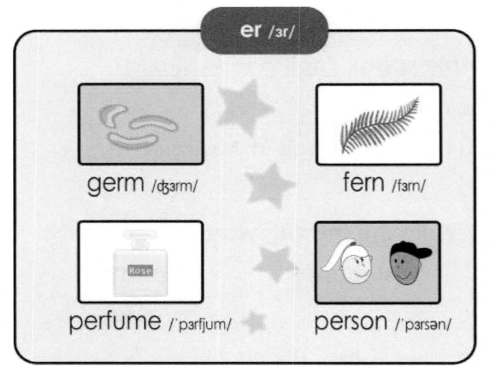

More words

serve

mermaid

Germany

herb

her

Write the words

er /ɜr/

Write the letters & Read the sentences!

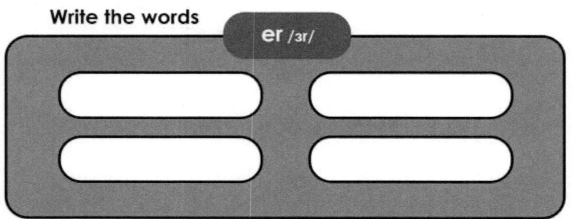

This p_ _fume is h_ _s.

We saw some f_ _ns in G_ _many.

That p_ _son is buying some h_ _bs.

Complete the words

1. P_____e   3. S_____h   5. A_____c

2. V_____e   4. H_____i   6. F_____h

Write the answer next to the letter "A"

A: ___ **7.** What language ___ people speak in France?

a. does
b. do
c. is

A: ___ **8.** They ___ Japanese in Japan. They ___ Arabic.

a. don't speak, speak
b. speak, dont' speak
c. speak, don't speak

A: ___ **9.** Do people speak Portuguese in Brazil?

a. Yes, they did.
b. Yes, I do.
c. Yes, they do.

A: ___ **10.** ___ German in Canada.

a. No body speaks
b. Nobody speaks
c. Nobody speak

Answers on Page 306

Lesson 27

- Learn the words
- Learn the sentences
- Learn the phonics
- Test yourself!

In the refrigerator

в холодильнику

Learn the words

1. milk
молоко

2. meat
м'ясо

3. bread
хліб

4. ice
лід

5. water
вода

6. cola
кола

7. tea
чай

8. salad
салат

9. juice
сік

10. ice cream
морозиво

Write the missing letters!

1. m_ _k

2. m_a_

3. b_e_ _

4. _c_

5. w_t_ _

6. c_l_

7. _e_

8. _al_d

9. j_ _ _e

10. i_e c_e_m

Have fun with the words!

1. need / I / bread / some / buy / to

   _____ .

2. to / milk / He / buy / any / doesn't / need

   _____ .

3. buy / this / week / to / Do / any / tea / you / need

   _____ ?

4. ice / don't / to / need / cream / any / I / buy

   _____ .

5. doesn't / need / cola / any / She / buy / to

   _____ .

6. at / supermarket / to / need / he / buy / What / the / does

   _____ ?

7. He / some / water / buy / needs / to

   _____ .

8. to / this / buy / Does / need / any / juice / she / week

   _____ ?

What do you need to buy at the supermarket?

I need to buy some <u>milk</u>.

I don't need to buy any <u>cola</u>.

Write the missing words!

What _____ you _____ to buy at the supermarket?

I _____ to buy _____ bread.

I _____ need _____ buy any _____ .

What does he need _____ buy _____ the _____ ?

_____ needs to _____ some _____ .

He doesn't need _____ buy _____ pizza.

What _____ she _____ to _____ at the _____ ?

She _____ to _____ some _____ .

_____ need _____ buy any _____ .

_____ ?

_____ .

_____ .

Do you need to buy any <u>salad</u> this week?

Yes, I need to buy some salad.

No, there's salad in the refrigerator.

Write the missing words!

Do you _____ to buy any ice _____ this week?

Yes, I _____ to _____ some _____ cream.

No, _____ ice cream in the _____ .

Does she need _____ buy any _____ this _____ ?

_____ , she needs to _____ some juice.

No, there's _____ in _____ refrigerator.

_____ he _____ to buy any _____ _____ week?

Yes, he _____ to buy _____ _____ .

_____ , _____ water _____ the _____ .

_____ ?

_____ .

_____ .

ir /ɜr/

bird /bɜrd/

shirt /ʃɜrt/

circle /ˈsɜrkəl/

first /fɜrst/

More words

girl

stir

firm

skirt

dirt

Write the words

ir /ɜr/

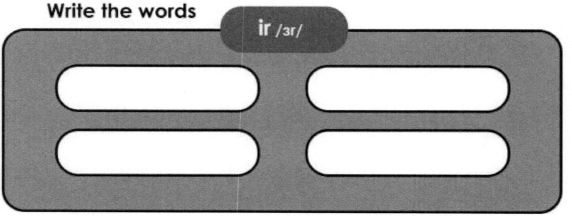

Write the letters & Read the sentences!

The g_ _l wore a pink sk_ _t.

There is some d_ _t on your sh_ _t.

We sat in a c_ _cle at my b_ _thday party.

Complete the words

1. b_____d   3. s_____d   5. m_____t

2. w_____r   4. j_____e   6. c_____a

Write the answer next to the letter "A"

A: ___ **7.** What ___ he ___ to buy at the supermarket?

a. does, needs
b. does, need
c. do, need

A: ___ **8.** I ___ to buy any ice.

a. need
b. doesn't need
c. don't need

A: ___ **9.** Do you need to buy any meat at the supermarket?

a. No, there's meat in the refrigerator.
b. No, theres meat in the refrigerator.
c. No, there's meat in refrigerator.

A: ___ **10.** ___ she need to buy any milk at the supermarket?

a. Is
b. Does
c. Do

Answers on Page 306

Lesson 28
- Learn the words
- Learn the sentences
- Learn the phonics
- Test yourself!

Desserts

десерти

Learn the words

1. **ice cream**
морозиво

2. **apple pie**
яблучний пиріг

3. **cheesecake**
сирний пиріг

4. **pudding**
пудинг

5. **cake**
торт

6. **cupcakes**
кекси

7. **brownies**
шоколадні тістечка

8. **pastries**
тістечка

9. **waffles**
вафлі

10. **cookies**
печиво

Write the missing letters!

1. i _ _ c _ e _ m

2. _ p _ le p _ _

3. ch _ _ se _ a _ e

4. p _ d _ i _ g

5. c _ k _

6. c _ p _ a _ e _

7. b _ o _ n _ es

8. p _ s _ ri _ s

9. w _ f _ l _ s

10. _ o _ k _ es

Have fun with the words!

Find the 8 desserts!

sausage chicken bedroom

Germany

carpet salad Chinese

Hindi cheesecake brownies

cupcakes shrimp floor juice

milk laundry

snake clothes pudding cookies

waffles turtle draw bacon

run

Japan computer meat

pastries salami surf England

cake

mouse write hamster

Write the 8 shapes

1.	3.	5.	7.
2.	4.	6.	8.

What did you have for dessert last night?

We had <u>cheesecake</u> for dessert.

We didn't have <u>brownies</u> for dessert.

Write the missing words!

What did you _____ for dessert _____ night?

We _____ apple _____ for dessert.

_____ didn't _____ ice _____ for _____.

What _____ he have _____ dessert last _____?

_____ had _____ for _____.

He _____ have _____ _____ dessert.

What _____ they _____ for _____ _____ night?

They _____ _____ for _____.

_____ didn't _____ waffles _____ _____.

_____?

_____.

_____.

Did you have <u>pudding</u> for dessert last night?

Yes, I did.

No, I didn't. I had <u>cupcakes</u>.

Write the missing words!

Did you have _____ for _____ last _____?

Yes, _____ _____.

_____, I didn't. I _____ cake.

Did she _____ cheesecake for _____ _____ night?

_____, she _____.

No, she _____. _____ had _____.

_____ they have _____ for _____ last _____?

Yes, _____ _____.

No, _____ . They _____ ice _____.

_____?

_____.

_____.

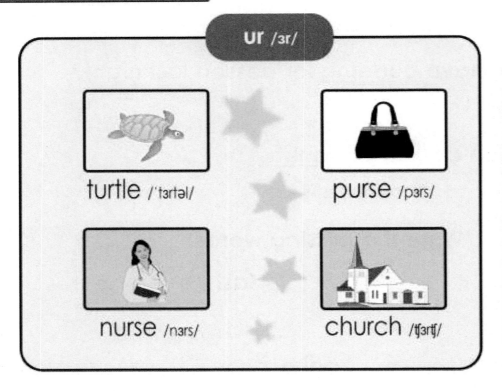

ur /ɜr/

turtle /ˈtɜrtəl/	purse /pɜrs/
nurse /nɜrs/	church /tʃɜrtʃ/

More words

turn

burn

surf

blur

hurt

Write the words

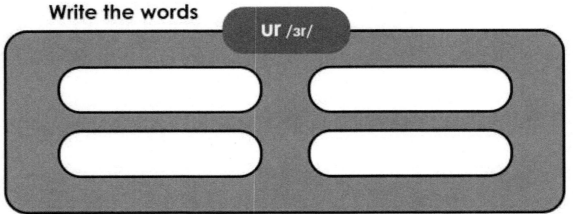

ur /ɜr/

Write the letters & Read the sentences!

The n_ _se helped me after I h_ _t my leg.

She forgot her p_ _se at the ch_ _ch.

I saw a t_ _tle while s_ _fing.

Complete the words

1. c_____s   3. a_____e 5. w_____s

2. p_____g   4. b_____s   6. p_____s

Write the answer next to the letter "A"

A: ___ **7.** What ___ you have ___ dessert last night?

a. did, of
b. do, for
c. did, for

A: ___ **8.** She didn't ___ cheesecake for dessert.

a. had
b. has
c. have

A: ___ **9.** Did they have pastries for dessert last night?

a. No, they didn't. They had cookies.
b. No, they did. They had cookies.
c. No, they didn't. They have cookies.

A: ___ **10.** Did they have pudding for dessert last night?

a. Yes, they do.
b. Yes, they did.
c. Yes they did.

Answers on Page 306

Lesson
29
- Learn the words
- Learn the sentences
- Learn the phonics
- Test yourself!

At school

в школі

Learn the words

1. **classroom**
   класна кімната

2. **nurse's office**
   кабінет медсестри

3. **hall**
   вестибюль

4. **gym**
   спортзал

5. **office**
   кабінет

6. **computer lab**
   комп'ютерний клас

7. **music room**
   музичний клас

8. **lunchroom**
   їдальня

9. **science lab**
   наукова лабораторія

10. **art room**
    художній зал

Write the missing letters!

1. c_a_sr_om

2. n_r_e's o_f_ce

3. h_l_

4. _y_

5. of_i_ _

6. c_m_ut_r la_

7. m_ _ic _o_m

8. l_n_hr_o_

9. s_ _en_e l_b

10. a_t r_ _m

Have fun with the words!

Write the 3 missing words

1._____

2. _____

3. _____

> classroom
>
> nurse's office
>
> science lab
>
> music room
>
> computer lab
>
> gym
>
> art room

1._____

2. _____

3. _____

> hall
>
> classroom
>
> art room
>
> science lab
>
> lunchroom
>
> office
>
> music room

1._____

2. _____

3. _____

> office
>
> hall
>
> computer lab
>
> gym
>
> classroom
>
> nurse's office
>
> lunchroom

1._____

2. _____

3. _____

> science lab
>
> art room
>
> gym
>
> music room
>
> hall
>
> lunchroom
>
> nurse's office

1._____

2. _____

3. _____

> office
>
> music room
>
> nurse's office
>
> classroom
>
> lunchroom
>
> computer lab
>
> gym

1._____

2. _____

3. _____

> computer lab
>
> office
>
> lunchroom
>
> hall
>
> science lab
>
> classroom
>
> art room

Where were you this morning?

I was in the <u>music room</u> this morning.

I wasn't in the <u>office</u>.

Write the missing words!

Where _____ you this _____?

I _____ in the _____ this _____.

I wasn't in _____ gym.

_____ was she _____ morning?

She _____ _____ the art _____ _____ morning.

_____ wasn't in _____ science _____.

Where _____ he _____ _____?

_____ was _____ the _____ room this _____.

He _____ in _____ _____.

_____ ?

_____ .

_____ .

Were you in the <u>lunchroom</u> this morning?

Yes, I was.

No, I wasn't. I was in the <u>hall</u>.

Write the missing words!

Were _____ in the computer _____ this _____?

_____ , I _____ .

No, _____ wasn't. I was _____ the _____ lab.

Was he in _____ classroom _____ morning?

Yes, _____ _____ .

_____ , he wasn't. He was _____ _____ gym.

_____ she in the _____ room this _____?

Yes, _____ _____ .

No, she _____ . She _____ in the _____ office.

_____?

_____.

_____.

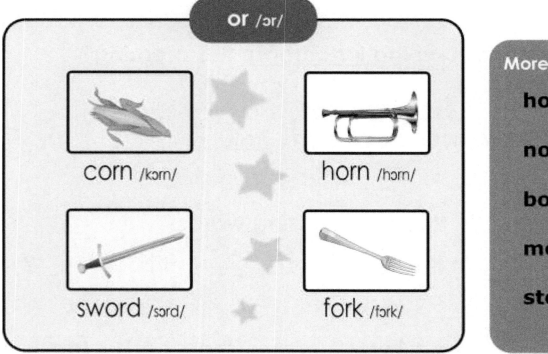

or /ɔr/

corn /kɔrn/

horn /hɔrn/

sword /sɔrd/

fork /fɔrk/

More words

horse

north

born

more

storm

Write the words

or /ɔr/

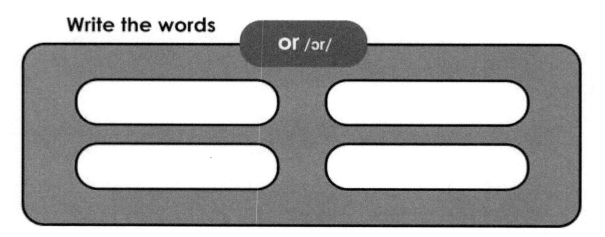

Write the letters & Read the sentences!

He used a f_ _k to eat the c_ _n.

A st_ _m is coming from the n_ _th.

M_ _e h_ _ses were b_ _n.

Complete the words

1. m_____ m   3. c_____ b   5. o_____ e

2. l_____ m   4. n_____ e   6. c_____ m

Write the answer next to the letter "A"

A: ___ **7.** Where ___ you this morning?

a. was
b. were
c. are

A: ___ **8.** I ___ the art room this morning.

a. were in
b. was at
c. was in

A: ___ **9.** Were you in the science lab this morning?

a. No, I weren't. I was in the gym.
b. No, I wasn't. I was in the gym.
c. No I wasn't. I was in the gym.

A: ___ **10.** ___ he in ___ this morning?

a. Was, the hall
b. Were, the hall
c. Was, hall

Answers on Page 306

Transportation

транспорт

Learn the words

1. **ride a motorcycle**
їздити на мотоциклі

2. **take an airplane**
летіти літаком

3. **take the ferry**
переправлятися на поромі

4. **take a taxi**
брати таксі

5. **catch a bus**
сідати на автобус

6. **ride a bike**
їздити на велосипеді

7. **take the subway**
їздити на метро

8. **ride a scooter**
їздити на скутері

9. **drive a car**
водити машину

10. **take a train**
їздити потягом

Write the missing letters!

1. r_d_ a mo_o_c_c_e

2. t_ _e a_ a_rpl_n_

3. t_k_ t_e f_r_y

4. _ak_ a t_x_

5. _a_c_ a b_s

6. _i_e a b_k_

7. _ak_ th_ s_b_a_

8. ri_ _ a sc_o_e_

9. d_i_e a _a_

10. _ _ke a tr_ _n

Have fun with the words!

take •	• a car
take •	• a train
ride •	• a bus
ride •	• a motorcycle
catch •	• a taxi
ride •	• the subway
drive •	• a bike
take •	• a scooter

Write the 2 missing transportations!

1. _____

2. _____

Unscramble the letters!

1. tmeoyorclc _____

2. crosoet _____

How do you go there on <u>Mondays</u>?

I always <u>catch a bus</u> on Mondays.

I never <u>take the train</u>.

Write the missing words!

How _____ you go _____ on Mondays?

I always _____ the subway on _____ .

I _____ drive a _____ .

How does _____ go there _____ Tuesdays?

He _____ rides _____ motorcycle on _____ .

He never rides a _____ .

How _____ she _____ there _____ _____?

She _____ _____ the ferry _____ Wednesdays.

She _____ _____ an _____ .

_____ ?

_____ .

_____ .

Does he <u>ride a scooter</u> there on <u>Sundays</u>?

Yes, he always does.

No, he never does. He always <u>rides a bike</u>.

Write the missing words!

Does _____ catch _____ bus _____ on Thursdays?

Yes, she always _____.

No, she _____ does. She always _____ a train.

Do _____ ride a _____ there on Fridays?

Yes, I _____.

_____, I never do. I _____ take a _____.

Do _____ _____ a scooter there _____ Saturdays?

_____, they _____ _____.

No, they _____ do. They _____ take _____ subway.

_____?

_____.

_____.

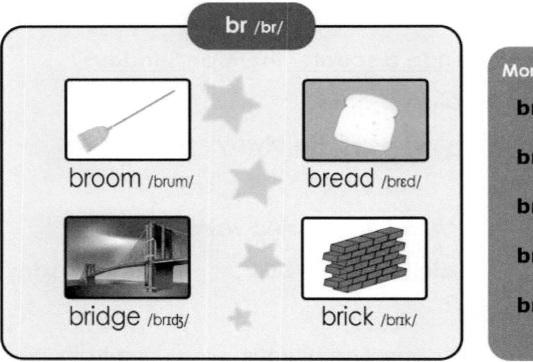

br /br/

broom /brum/

bread /brɛd/

bridge /brɪdʒ/

brick /brɪk/

More words

brain

bring

break

brown

bright

Write the words

br /br/

Write the letters & Read the sentences!

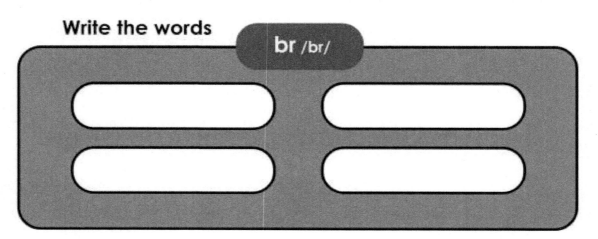

The _ _idge is made with _ _icks.

_ _ad likes to eat _ _own _ _ead.

I can _ _ing a _ _oom.

Complete the words

1. f_____y

3. s_____y

5. t_____n

2. a_____e

4. m_____e

6. s_____r

Write the answer next to the letter "A"

A: ___ **7.** How do you go there on Sundays?

a. I always catch a bus at Sundays.
b. I alway ride a scooter on Sundays.
c. I always take the subway on Sundays.

A: ___ **8.** He never ___ a motorcycle.

a. riding
b. rides
c. ride

A: ___ **9.** Does she take the subway on Fridays?

a. Yes, she never does.
b. Yes, she always does.
c. Yes, she always dose.

A: ___ **10.** Do you ___ there on Mondays?

a. take a taxi
b. drive a motorcycle
c. take a airplane

Answers on Page 306

Lesson
31
- Learn the words
- Learn the sentences
- Learn the phonics
- Test yourself!

Fast food

фастфуд

Learn the words

1. **a cheeseburger**
Чізбургер

2. **onion rings**
цибулеві кільця

3. **fried chicken**
смажена курка

4. **chicken nuggets**
курячі нагетси

5. **french fries**
картопля фрі

6. **a taco**
тако

7. **a burrito**
буріто

8. **a pancake**
млинець

9. **a doughnut**
пончик

10. **a hot dog**
хот дог

Write the missing letters!

1. a c_ee_eb_r_e_

2. o_i_n r_n_s

3. _r_ _d c_ic_e_

4. ch_c_ _n n_g_e_s

5. f_e_c_ f_i_s

6. a t_ _ _

7. a b_r_i_o

8. a p_n_a_ _

9. a d_u_h_ut

10. a h_t d_ _

Have fun with the words!

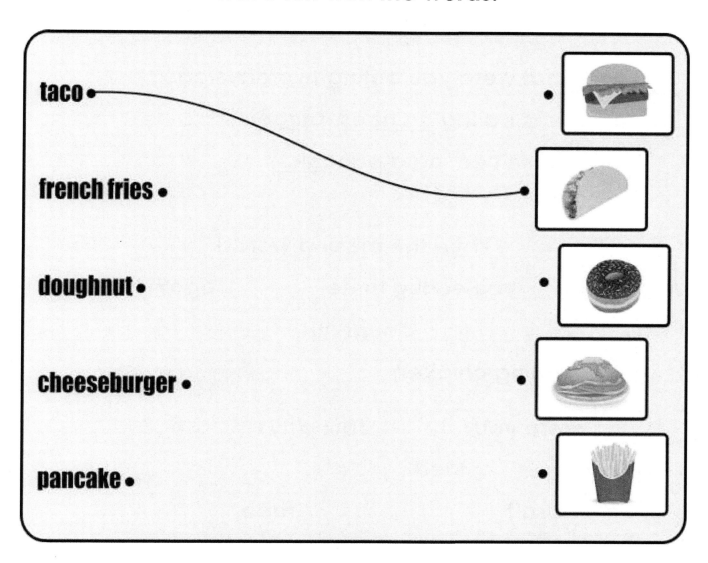

Write 4 more fast foods!

1. _____   3. _____

2. _____   4. _____

What were you eating?

_____

What were you eating <u>two</u> days ago?

I was eating <u>a cheeseburger</u>.

I wasn't eating <u>a pancake</u>.

Write the missing words!

What _____ you eating three _____ ago?

I was _____ _____ doughnut.

I _____ eating chicken _____ .

_____ were you _____ four days _____ ?

I _____ _____ fried _____ .

_____ wasn't _____ _____ taco.

What _____ _____ eating _____ days _____ ?

I _____ _____ _____ hot _____ .

_____ _____ _____ onion _____ .

_____ _____ ?

_____ _____ .

_____ _____ .

Were you eating <u>a burrito</u> <u>four</u> days ago?

Yes, I was.

No, I wasn't. I was eating <u>chicken nuggets</u>.

Write the missing words!

Were you _____ a taco _____ days _____?

Yes, I _____.

No, _____ wasn't. I _____ eating _____ fries.

_____ you _____ a pancake seven _____ ago?

Yes, _____ was.

No, I _____. I _____ _____ a _____ dog.

_____ you _____ _____ rings _____ days ago?

Yes, _____ _____.

_____, I _____. I _____ _____ fried _____.

_____?

_____.

_____.

Learn the phonics

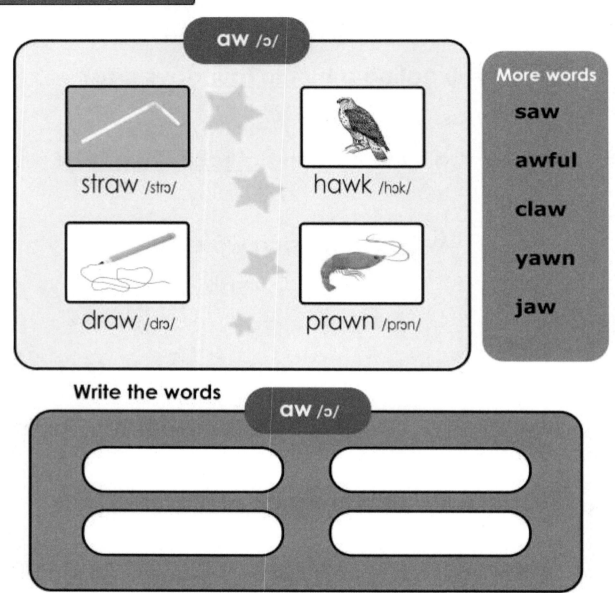

aw /ɔ/

straw /strɔ/

hawk /hɔk/

draw /drɔ/

prawn /prɔn/

More words

saw

awful

claw

yawn

jaw

Write the words

aw /ɔ/

Write the letters & Read the sentences!

The h_ _k has big cl_ _s.

I s_ _ some pr_ _ns.

His j_ _ opens wide when he y_ _ns.

Complete the words

1. d_____t   3. f_____s 5. p_____e

2. c_____r   4. o_____s 6. b_____o

Write the answer next to the letter "A"

A: ___ **7.** What ___ you ___ two days ago?

a. were, eat
b. was, eating
c. were, eating

A: ___ **8.** I ___ eating chicken nuggets.

a. were
b. weren't
c. wasn't

A: ___ **9.** Were you eating a taco five days ago?

a. No, I wasn't. I was eaten a hot dog.
b. No, I wasnt. I was eating hot dog.
c. No, I wasn't. I was eating a hot dog.

A: ___ **10.** Were you eating fried ___ three ___ ago?

a. chicken, days
b. nuggets, days
c. chicken, day

Answers on Page 306

Lesson 32

- Learn the words
- Learn the sentences
- Learn the phonics
- Test yourself!

Landscapes

пейзажі

Learn the words

1. **mountain**
   гора

2. **forest**
   ліс

3. **beach**
   пляж

4. **river**
   річка

5. **volcano**
   вулкан

6. **island**
   острів

7. **jungle**
   джунглі

8. **waterfall**
   водоспад

9. **lake**
   озеро

10. **ocean**
    океан

Write the missing letters!

1. m_ _n_a_n

2. f_re_ _

3. b_ _c_

4. r_ _e_

5. v_l_a_o

6. i_l_n_

7. _u_g_e

8. w_ _e_fa_l

9. l_ _ _

10. o_e_ _

Have fun with the words!

Word Search

```
n u i j g l c p y l a k e e y w n s
z x c c f s f n e t z t z v q a q b
r l c l l o f b c j r a e u a t e b
g z a x j i r h h n a m l o v e k e
i s c a j s z e o w d o p v o r y a
u l y m u l j t s j c u y r l f m c
i r o i n a l b y t e n s l c a a h
o g c r g n o r i b u t p z a l v i
n l e d l d j d z o t a p h n l x f
v p a e e g d b q b p i d w o v e t
a r n p z r i v e r d n z z z n m s
a r a q k h n x k z c s e e g z u h
```

Word directions:

beach	**waterfall**
mountain	**island**
forest	**jungle**
river	**lake**
volcano	**ocean**

Where were you walking to yesterday?

Yesterday, we were walking to the <u>beach</u>.

We weren't walking to the <u>waterfall</u>.

Write the missing words!

Where _____ you walking _____ yesterday?

_____ , we were _____ to _____ forest.

We _____ walking _____ the _____ .

_____ were they _____ to _____ ?

Yesterday, _____ _____ walking to _____ jungle.

They weren't _____ to _____ _____ .

Where _____ you _____ _____ ?

_____ , _____ were _____ _____ the _____ .

We _____ _____ to _____ mountain.

_____ ?

_____ .

_____ .

Were they walking to the <u>river</u> yesterday?

Yes, they were.

No, they were walking to the <u>lake</u>.

Write the missing words!

Were they _____ to the _____ yesterday?

Yes, they _____ .

No, _____ were walking to _____ jungle.

_____ you walking _____ the ocean _____ ?

_____ , _____ were.

No, we _____ _____ to the _____ .

_____ they _____ _____ the volcano _____ ?

Yes, _____ _____ .

_____ , they _____ walking _____ the _____ .

_____ ?

_____ .

_____ .

cl /kl/

clam /klæm/

clap /klæp/

clothes /klouðz/

clock /klɑk/

More words

clown

class

club

clever

climb

Write the words

cl /kl/

Write the letters & Read the sentences!

The people _ _apped for the _ _own.

This _ _ass is about _ _ocks.

I _ _imbed a tree and saw some _ _othes.

Complete the words

1. m_____n   3. r_____r   5. o_____n

2. b_____h   4. j_____e   6. w_____l

Write the answer next to the letter "A"

A: ___ **7.** Where were you walking to yesterday?

a. I were walking to the forest.
b. We were walking to the forest.
c. We was walking to the forest.

A: ___ **8.** They ___ walking to the volcano.

a. werent'
b. wasn't
c. weren't

A: ___ **9.** Were you walking to the lake yesterday?

a. No, we were walking to the island.
b. No, they were walking to the island.
c. No, we were walking to island.

A: ___ **10.** Were they ___ to the ocean?

a. walk
b. walking
c. walks

Answers on Page 306

- Learn the words
- Learn the sentences
- Learn the phonics
- Test yourself!

Homework

домашнє завдання

Learn the words

1. **workbook**
збірник вправ

2. **vocabulary words**
лексика

3. **quiz**
вікторина

4. **science project**
науковий проект

5. **speech**
вимова

6. **article**
стаття

7. **poster**
плакат

8. **presentation**
презентація

9. **essay**
есе

10. **report**
звіт

Write the missing letters!

1. w _ r _ b _ o _

2. vo _ a _ u _ a _ y w _ _ ds

3. _ u _ _

4. s _ i _ n _ e p _ o _ e _ t

5. s _ _ e _ h

6. a _ t _ c _ e

7. p _ s _ _ r

8. p _ e _ e _ t _ o _

9. e _ s _ _

10. r _ _ or _

- 198 -

Have fun with the words!

Find the 8 homework words!

sausage quiz bedroom

chicken nuggets

ocean

pancake salad mountain

jungle beach essay taco

doughnut article lake

workbook

clothes presentation report

draw

waffles burrito bacon

forest

speech cheeseburger meat

pastries

poster surf

essay fries

french write waterfall

Write the 8 shapes

1.	3.	5.	7.
2.	4.	6.	8.

Which homework have you already done?

I have already done the <u>report</u>.

However, I haven't done the <u>quiz</u> yet.

Write the missing words!

Which _____ have _____ already _____?

I _____ already done _____ presentation.

However, I _____ _____ the _____ words yet.

_____ homework _____ you _____ done?

I have _____ _____ the _____.

However, I _____ done _____ poster _____.

Which _____ _____ you _____ _____?

I _____ already _____ _____ science _____.

_____, I _____ _____ the _____ _____.

_____?

_____.

_____.

Have you done the <u>speech</u> yet?

Yes, I have already done it.

No, I haven't done it yet.

Write the missing words!

Have you _____ the workbook _____ ?

Yes, _____ have already _____ it.

No, I _____ done _____ yet.

_____ you _____ the article _____ ?

Yes, _____ have _____ done it.

_____ , I _____ done _____ yet.

Have _____ _____ _____ yet?

_____ , I _____ already _____ _____ .

No, I _____ _____ it _____ .

_____?

_____.

_____.

Learn the phonics

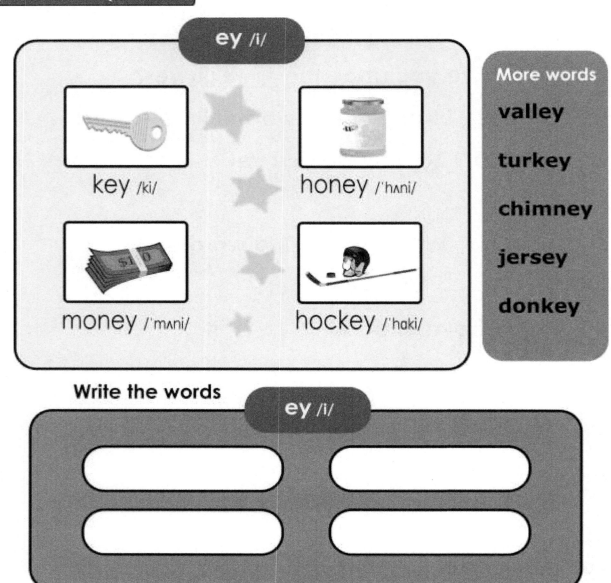

ey /i/

key /ki/	honey /ˈhʌni/
money /ˈmʌni/	hockey /ˈhaki/

More words

valley

turkey

chimney

jersey

donkey

Write the words

ey /i/

Write the letters & Read the sentences!

This jers_ _ is for the hock_ _ game.

There is a donk_ _ in the vall_ _.

That hon_ _ costs a lot of mon_ _.

Complete the words

1. a_____e   3. q_____z   5. s_____h

2. p_____n   4. w_____k   6. r_____t

Write the answer next to the letter "A"

A: ___ **7.** Which homework ___ you already ___?

a. have, did
b. has, done
c. have, done

A: ___ **8.** However, I ___ done the quiz ___.

a. haven't, already
b. have, yet
c. haven't, yet

A: ___ **9.** Have you ___ the poster yet? Yes, I have already done ___.

a. did, it
b. done, it
c. done, yet

A: ___ **10.** Have you done the science project yet?

a. No, I haven't done it yet.
b. No, I have done it yet.
c. No, I haven't already done it.

Answers on Page 306

Lesson 34

- Learn the words
- Learn the sentences
- Learn the phonics
- Test yourself!

The calendar

календар

Learn the words

1. class заняття	**6. test** тест
2. birthday день народження	**7. meeting** зібрання
3. party вечірка	**8. recital** концерт
4. competition змагання	**9. appointment** зустріч
5. speech виступ	**10. day off** вихідний

Write the missing letters!

1. _i_t_d_ _   6. m_e_i_ _

2. p_ _t_   7. r_c_t_l

3. c_m_e_it_on   8. a_p_i_t_e_t

4. c_ _s_   9. t_ _ _

5. s_ _e_h   10. _ _y o_f

Have fun with the words!

birthday
party
competition
class
speech

meeting
recital
appointment
test
day off

r
e
c
i
t
a
l

Write the missing word:

_____

When is your <u>brother</u>'s <u>birthday</u>?

My brother's birthday is on the <u>second</u> of <u>June</u>.

He hasn't prepared for his birthday yet.

Write the missing words!

When is _____ father's _____?

My _____ appointment is _____ the _____ of May.

He hasn't _____ for _____ appointment _____.

_____ _____ your _____ recital?

My friend's _____ is on _____ third _____ July.

She _____ prepared _____ _____ recital yet.

When _____ _____ sister's _____?

_____ _____ test is _____ the twentieth of _____.

She _____ prepared _____ _____ test _____.

_____?

_____.

_____.

Is your <u>aunt</u>'s <u>party</u> on the <u>first</u> of <u>February</u>?

Yes, her party is on that day.

No, my aunt has a <u>speech</u> on that day.

Write the missing words!

Is _____ mother's _____ on the tenth of _____ ?

Yes, _____ meeting is on _____ day.

No, my _____ has a _____ off on that _____ .

_____ your _____ class on the _____ of April?

Yes, his _____ is _____ that day.

_____ , my uncle _____ a _____ on that day.

Is _____ grandma's party _____ the _____ of May?

_____ , her _____ is _____ that _____ .

No, _____ has a _____ on _____ day.

_____ ?

_____ .

_____ .

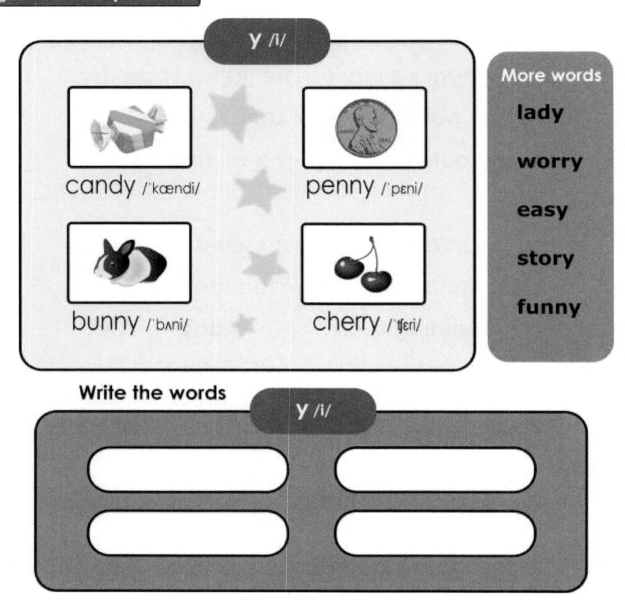

y /i/

candy /ˈkændi/

penny /ˈpɛni/

bunny /ˈbʌni/

cherry /ˈtʃɛri/

More words

lady

worry

easy

story

funny

Write the words

y /i/

Write the letters & Read the sentences!

This stor_ is reall_ funn_.

The lad_ ate the cherr_.

It is not eas_ to draw a bunn_.

Complete the words

1. m_____g

3. p_____y

5. b_____y

2. a_____t

4. r_____l

6. c_____n

Write the answer next to the letter "A"

A: ___ **7.** When is ___ father's day off?

a. you're
b. your
c. you

A: ___ **8.** My aunt's appointment is ___ the third of October.

a. at
b. in
c. on

A: ___ **9.** She ___ prepared for her test yet.

a. hasn't
b. haven't
c. has

A: ___ **10.** Is your brother's class on the thirteenth of November?

a. Yes, her class is on that day.
b. Yes, his class isn't on that day.
c. Yes, his class is on that day.

Answers on Page 306

Lesson 35

- Learn the words
- Learn the sentences
- Learn the phonics
- Test yourself!

Camping

кемпінг

Learn the words

1. **a barbecue**
   барбекю

2. **a gas bottle**
   газовий балон

3. **sleeping bags**
   спальні мішки

4. **plastic dishes**
   пластиковий посуд

5. **fishing rods**
   вудки

6. **binoculars**
   бінокль

7. **a flashlight**
   ліхтарики

8. **a tent**
   намет

9. **a compass**
   компас

10. **a cooler**
    портативный холодильник

Write the missing letters!

1. b _ r _ e _ u _

2. g _ _ b _ t _le

3. s _ e _ pi _ g b _ _ s

4. p _ a _ t c d _ s _ e _

5. f _ s _ i _ g r _ _ s

6. b _ n _ cu _ a _ s

7. f _ a _ h _ i _ _ t

8. t _ _ _

9. c _ _ p _ s _

10. co _ l _ _

- 210 -

Have fun with the words!

Write the 3 missing words

1._____

2. _____

3. _____

> barbecue
>
> gas bottle
>
> sleeping bags
>
> compass
>
> plastic dishes
>
> flashlight
>
> cooler

1._____

2. _____

3. _____

> sleeping bags
>
> tent
>
> plastic dishes
>
> binoculars
>
> compass
>
> fishing rods
>
> barbecue

1._____

2. _____

3. _____

> cooler
>
> gas bottle
>
> flashlight
>
> plastic dishes
>
> fishing rods
>
> binoculars
>
> tent

1._____

2. _____

3. _____

> compass
>
> tent
>
> fishing rods
>
> barbecue
>
> cooler
>
> binoculars
>
> flashlight

1._____

2. _____

3. _____

> barbecue
>
> sleeping bags
>
> cooler
>
> tent
>
> flashlight
>
> plastic dishes
>
> gas bottle

1._____

2. _____

3. _____

> plastic dishes
>
> compass
>
> gas bottle
>
> sleeping bags
>
> binoculars
>
> fishing rods
>
> barbecue

What has he packed for the camping trip?

He has already packed <u>binoculars</u>.

However, he hasn't packed <u>a tent</u> yet.

Write the missing words!

What has he _____ for the _____ trip?

He _____ already packed _____ flashlight.

However, _____ hasn't packed _____ bags _____ .

What _____ she _____ for the camping _____ ?

_____ has _____ packed _____ dishes.

However, she _____ _____ a _____ yet.

_____ has he _____ for _____ camping _____ ?

He _____ already _____ _____ gas _____ .

_____ , he _____ packed _____ cooler _____ .

_____ ?

_____ .

_____ .

Has she packed <u>a barbecue</u> yet?

Yes, she already has.

No, she hasn't yet.

Write the missing words!

Has she _____ a _____ yet?

Yes, _____ already _____ .

_____ , she hasn't _____ .

Has _____ packed _____ rods _____ ?

Yes, _____ already has.

_____ , he _____ yet.

_____ she _____ a _____ bottle _____ ?

_____ , _____ _____ has.

No, _____ _____ .

_____ ?

_____ .

_____ .

Learn the phonics

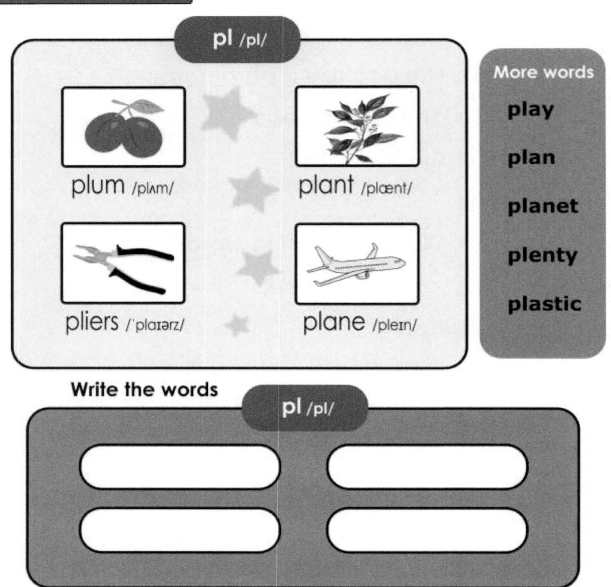

pl /pl/

plum /plʌm/

plant /plænt/

pliers /ˈplaɪərz/

plane /pleɪn/

More words

play

plan

planet

plenty

plastic

Write the words

pl /pl/

Write the letters & Read the sentences!

There are _ _enty of _ _ums by the _ _ant.

The toy _ _ane is made of _ _astic.

I _ _an to buy some new _ _iers.

Complete the words

1. b_____s   3. p_____s   5.   c_____r

2. c_____s   4. g_____e   6.   b_____e

Write the answer next to the letter "A"

A: ___ **7.** What ___ she packed ___ the camping trip?

a. has, of
b. have, for
c. has, for

A: ___ **8.** He has already ___ the sleeping bags.

a. packed
b. packs
c. pack

A: ___ **9.** Has she packed a tent yet?

a. Yes, he already has.
b. No, she hasn't already.
c. Yes, she already has.

A: ___ **10.** Has he packed a ___ yet?

a. flashlight
b. sleeping bags
c. fishing rods

Answers on Page 306

Lesson 36

- Learn the words
- Learn the sentences
- Learn the phonics
- Test yourself!

Daily life

повсякденне життя

Learn the words

1. **woken up**
   прокинулись

2. **brushed my teeth**
   почистили зуби

3. **done homework**
   зробили домашнє завдання

4. **taken out the trash**
   викинули сміття

5. **cooked dinner**
   приготували обід

6. **eaten breakfast**
   поснідали

7. **gone to school**
   пішли до школи

8. **taken a shower**
   прийняли душ

9. **gone shopping**
   пішли за покупками

10. **gone to sleep**
    пішли спати

Write the missing letters!

1. w_k_n u_

2. b_u_h_d m_t_e _ _

3. d_n_ h_m_w _ _ k

4. t_k_n o_t t_e t_a_ _

5. c_o_e_ d_n_e_

6. _a_ _n b_e_k_a_t

7. g_ _e_t _s_h_o_

8. t_ _e_ a_s_o_e_

9. _on_ s_o_p_n_

10. g_n_ t_ s_ _e_

Have fun with the words!

1. brushed / already / teeth / had / I / my

   _____ .

2. trash / the / taken / yet / out / hadn't / She

   _____ .

3. he / had / done / already / What / o'clock / ten / by

   _____ ?

4. already / They / to / gone / school / had

   _____ .

5. hadn't / shower / yet / a / I / taken

   _____ .

6. already / sleep / to / she / Had / gone

   _____ ?

7. up / he / yet / hadn't / woken / No

   _____ .

8. shopping / they / gone / Had / already

   _____ ?

What had you already done by <u>eight</u> o'clock?

I had already <u>brushed my teeth</u>.

I hadn't <u>taken out the trash</u> yet.

Write the missing words!

What _____ you already _____ by _____ o'clock?

I had _____ woken _____ .

I _____ _____ a shower _____ .

_____ had he _____ done _____ nine _____ ?

He _____ already _____ homework.

_____ hadn't _____ _____ sleep yet.

What _____ she _____ _____ by _____ o'clock?

_____ had _____ _____ shopping.

She _____ _____ dinner _____ .

_____ ?

_____ .

_____ .

Had you already <u>gone shopping</u>?

Yes, I already had.

No, I hadn't gone shopping yet.

Write the missing words!

Had you _____ taken _____ the _____?

_____, I _____ had.

No, I _____ out _____ trash yet.

Had _____ brushed her _____?

_____, she already _____.

No, _____ hadn't _____ her teeth _____.

_____ he already _____ school?

Yes, _____.

_____, he _____ gone _____ school _____.

_____?

_____.

_____.

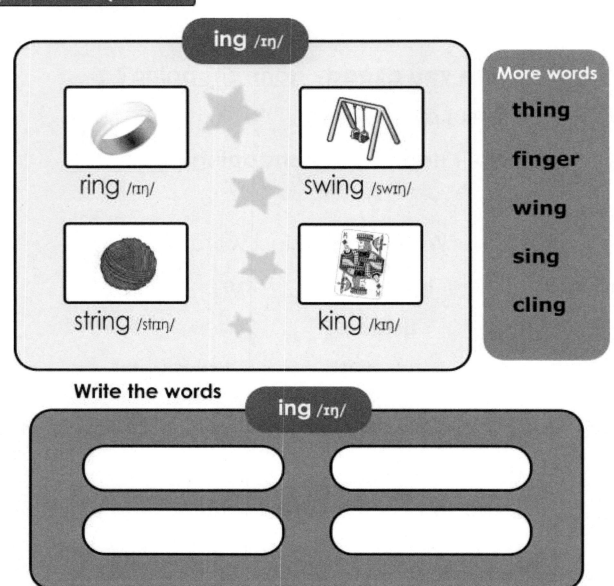

ing /ɪŋ/

ring /rɪŋ/

swing /swɪŋ/

string /strɪŋ/

king /kɪŋ/

More words

thing

finger

wing

sing

cling

Write the words

ing /ɪŋ/

Write the letters & Read the sentences!

This r_ _ _ is too small for my f_ _ _er.

The boy cl_ _ _s to the sw_ _ _.

The k_ _ _ can s_ _ _ very well.

Complete the words

1. t _____ h   3. s _____ r   5. h _____ k

2. b _____ t   4. s _____ g   6. d _____ r

Write the answer next to the letter "A"

A: ___ **7.** What had you already ___ by nine o'clock?

a. did
b. done
c. doing

A: ___ **8.** She ___ gone to school yet.

a. haven't
b. had
c. hadn't

A: ___ **9.** Had you already ___ up?

a. gone
b. taken
c. woken

A: ___ **10.** Had you already cooked dinner?

a. No, I hadn't eaten dinner yet.
b. No, I hadn't cooked dinner yet.
c. No, I had cooked dinner yet.

Answers on Page 306

- Learn the words
- Learn the sentences
- Learn the phonics
- Test yourself!

On the street

на вулиці

Learn the words

1. **a bus**
автобус

2. **a truck**
вантажівка

3. **an ambulance**
швидка допомога

4. **a fire engine**
пожежна машина

5. **some traffic lights**
кілька світлофорів

6. **a fire hydrant**
пожежний гідрант

7. **a stop sign**
знак зупинки

8. **a trash can**
сміттєвий бак

9. **some shops**
кілька магазинів

10. **a police car**
поліцейський автомобіль

Write the missing letters!

1. a _u_

2. a t_u_ _

3. a_ a_b l_n_e

4. a _ir_e_g_ _e

5. _o_e t_a_f_c li_h_s

6. a f_ _e h_d_a_t

7. a s_o_ s_ _n

8. a t_a_h c_ _

9. s_m_s_o_s

10. a po_i_ _ c_ _

Have fun with the words!

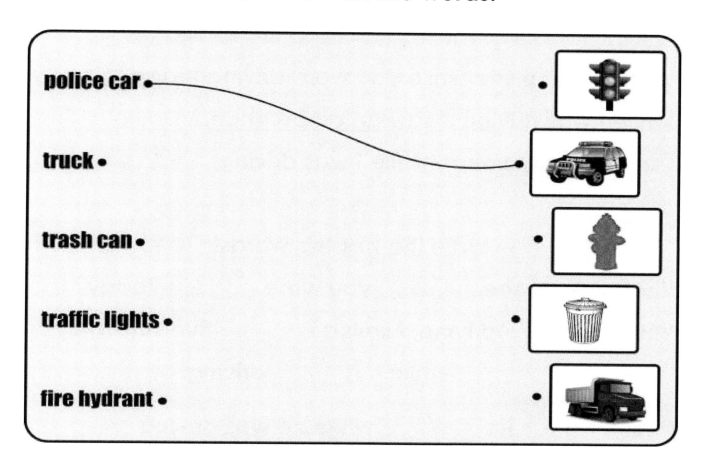

Unscramble the letters!

1. BSU _____

2. IREF NEGIEN _____

3. HPSOS _____

4. MBALAECUN _____

5. TSPO GINS _____

What did you see while you were driving today?

While I was driving, I saw <u>an ambulance</u>.

I saw an ambulance while I was driving.

Write the missing words!

What did you see _____ you were _____ today?

While I _____ driving, I saw a _____ hydrant.

I saw a fire _____ while I _____ driving.

What _____ he _____ while he was driving _____?

_____ he was _____, he saw some _____ lights.

He saw _____ traffic _____ while he was _____.

What did _____ see _____ she was _____ today?

While she _____ driving, she _____ a police _____.

_____ saw a _____ car _____ she _____ driving.

_____ ?

_____ .

_____ .

Did you see <u>a truck</u> while you were driving?

Yes, I did. I saw <u>two</u> trucks.

No, I didn't. I didn't see any.

Write the missing words!

Did _____ see an _____ while you _____ driving?

Yes, I _____ . I saw _____ ambulance.

No, I _____ . I didn't see _____ .

Did she see a stop _____ while _____ was _____ ?

Yes, _____ did. She _____ three _____ signs.

_____ , I didn't. I _____ _____ any.

_____ he see a _____ while he _____ _____ ?

Yes, _____ . He _____ _____ buses.

No, _____ didn't. He _____ see _____ .

_____ ?

_____ .

_____ .

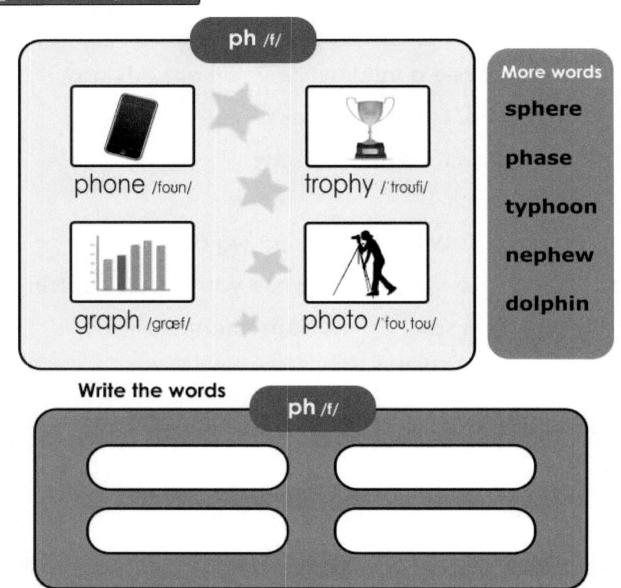

ph /f/

phone /foun/

trophy /ˈtroufi/

graph /græf/

photo /ˈfou͵tou/

More words

sphere

phase

typhoon

nephew

dolphin

Write the words

ph /f/

Write the letters & Read the sentences!

My ne_ _ew wants a _ _one.

I took a _ _oto of a dol_ _in.

This gra_ _ is about ty_ _oons.

Complete the words

1. t _____ n   3. f _____ t   5. a _____ e

2. s _____ n   4. p _____ r   6. t _____ k

Write the answer next to the letter "A"

A: ___ **7.** What ___ you see while you ___ driving today?

a. did, was
b. do, were
c. did, were

A: ___ **8.** While he was ___ he saw some traffic lights.

a. driving
b. driving,
c. driven,

A: ___ **9.** Did you see a fire engine while you were driving?

a. Yes, I did. I saw three fire engine.
b. Yes, I did. I saw one fire engine.
c. No, I did. I didn't see any.

A: ___ **10.** Did she see an ___ while she was driving?

a. ambulance
b. police car
c. bus

Answers on Page 306

Lesson 38
- Learn the words
- Learn the sentences
- Learn the phonics
- Test yourself!

Hobbies

хобі

Learn the words

1. **listen to music**
слухати музику

2. **play video games**
грати у відео ігри

3. **take photographs**
Фотографувати

4. **do some gardening**
займатися садівництвом

5. **go hiking**
відправлятися в піший похід

6. **sing karaoke**
співати в караоке

7. **go fishing**
рибалити

8. **watch movies**
дивитися фільми

9. **go camping**
відправлятися в похід з палатками

10. **play chess**
грати в шахи

Write the missing letters!

1. l s_e_ t_ m si_

2. p_a_ v_d_ _ g_m_s

3. t_ _e p_o_o ra_hs

4. d_ s_ _e g_r_e_i_g

5. _o h_ _i_g

6. s_ _g k_r_o_e

7. _o f_s_i_g

8. wa_c_ m_v_ _s

9. g_ c_m_ _n_

10. p_ _y c_e_ _

Have fun with the words!

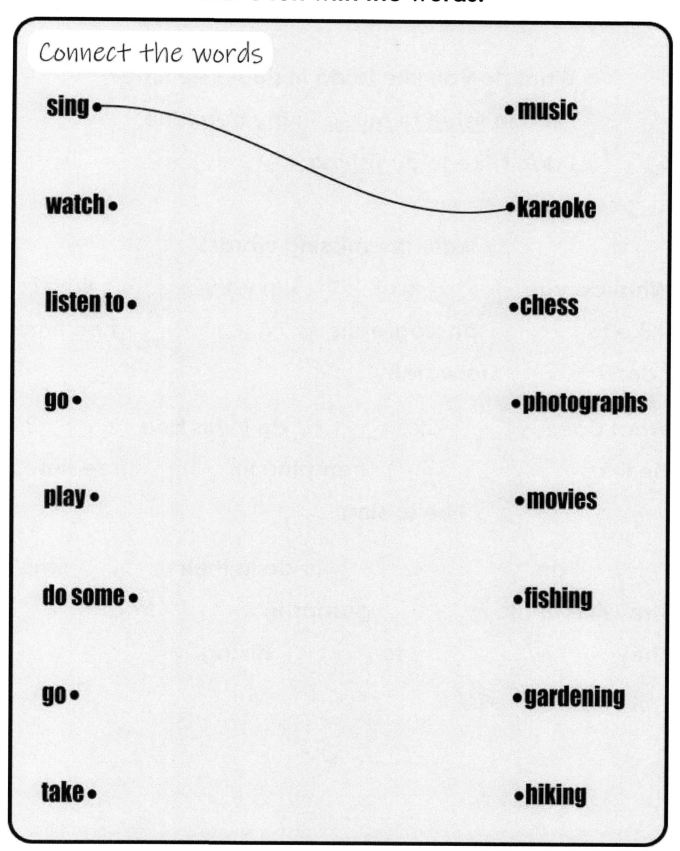

Connect the words

sing •   • music

watch •   • karaoke

listen to •   • chess

go •   • photographs

play •   • movies

do some •   • fishing

go •   • gardening

take •   • hiking

What do you like to do in your free time?

I like to <u>listen to music</u> in my free time.

I don't like to <u>go fishing</u>.

Write the missing words!

What do you _____ to _____ in your _____ time?

I like to _____ photographs _____ _____ free time.

I don't _____ to watch _____ .

What does _____ like _____ do in his free _____?

He likes _____ _____ camping in _____ free time.

_____ _____ like to sing _____ .

_____ do _____ _____ to do in their _____ time?

They like to play _____ games in _____ free _____ .

They _____ _____ to _____ hiking.

_____ ?

_____ .

_____ .

Do you like to <u>do some gardening</u> in your free time?

Yes, I really like to do some gardening.

No, I don't. I like to <u>play chess</u>.

Write the missing words!

Do you like to _____ to music in _____ free _____?

Yes, I _____ like _____ listen to _____.

No, I _____. I _____ to _____ movies.

Does he _____ to play _____ in _____ free time?

_____, he really _____ to _____ chess.

No, _____ doesn't. He likes _____ go _____.

Do they _____ to sing _____ in _____ free time?

Yes, _____ like to _____ karaoke.

_____, they _____. _____ to go _____.

_____?

_____.

_____.

Learn the phonics

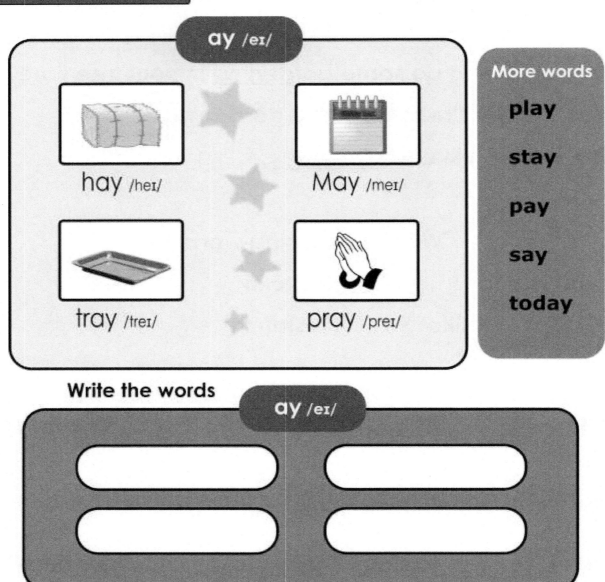

ay /eɪ/

hay /heɪ/

May /meɪ/

tray /treɪ/

pray /preɪ/

More words

play

stay

pay

say

today

Write the words

ay /eɪ/

Write the letters & Read the sentences!

I will p_ _ for the h_ _ tod_ _.

You can st_ _ here in M_ _.

They s_ _ to pr_ _ every d_ _.

Complete the words

1. g_____ g   3. k_____ e   5. c_____ g

2. p_____ s   4. f_____ g   6. h_____ g

Write the answer next to the letter "A"

A: ___ **7.** What do you like to do ___ your free time?

a. in
b. on
c. at

A: ___ **8.** I like to listen ___ music in ___ free time.

a. to, me
b. to, my
c. the, my

A: ___ **9.** He ___ like to go fishing.

a. don't
b. didn't
c. doesn't

A: ___ **10.** Does she like to watch movies in her free time?

a. No, she doesn't. She likes to watch movies.
b. No, she doesn't. She like to play chess.
c. No, she doesn't. She likes to listen to music.

Answers on Page 306

Lesson 39

- Learn the words
- Learn the sentences
- Learn the phonics
- Test yourself!

In the bedroom

в спальні

Learn the words

1. **pillow**
подушка

2. **bed**
ліжко

3. **blanket**
ковдра

4. **drawers**
шухляди

5. **mattress**
матрац

6. **alarm clock**
будильник

7. **lamp**
лампа

8. **bed sheets**
простирадло

9. **nightstand**
тумбочка

10. **wardrobe**
гардероб

Write the missing letters!

1. p_l_o_

2. b_ _

3. b_a_k_ _

4. d_a_e_s

5. m_t_r_s_

6. a_a_m _lo_ _

7. _a_ _

8. _e_s_e_ _s

9. n_ _h_st_n_

10. w_ _d_o_e

Have fun with the words!

➢ **Find one mistake and write the sentence correctly**

Why is you going shopping now?

_____

I'm going shopping because I need a new bed sheets.

_____

My bed sheets is already ten years old.

_____

Why is she go shopping now?

_____

She's going shopping because she need a new pillow.

_____

Her pillow are already twelve years old.

_____

Are they gone to buy a new pillow?

_____

Yes, they are. My pillow is too old.

_____

Why are you going shopping now?

I'm going shopping because I need a new <u>lamp</u>.

My lamp is already <u>eight</u> years old.

Write the missing words!

Why _____ you _____ shopping _____?

I'm going _____ _____ I need a new _____ clock.

My alarm _____ is already five _____ old.

_____ is _____ _____ shopping now?

He's going _____ because he _____ new _____.

_____ drawers are _____ eleven years _____.

Why _____ they _____ _____ now?

They're going _____ _____ they _____ a new bed.

Their _____ _____ already _____ years _____.

_____?

_____.

_____.

Are you going to buy a new <u>nightstand</u>?

Yes, I am. My nightstand is too old.

No, I'm not. I don't need a new one.

Write the missing words!

Are you _____ to buy a _____ blanket?

Yes, I _____. My blanket is _____ old.

No, I'm _____. I _____ need _____ new one.

_____ she going to _____ a new _____?

Yes, _____ is. _____ wardrobe is too _____.

No, _____ not. She doesn't need a new _____.

_____ they _____ to _____ new _____ sheets?

Yes, _____ . _____ bed _____ are too old.

_____ , they're not. They _____ need _____ ones.

_____ ?

_____ .

_____ .

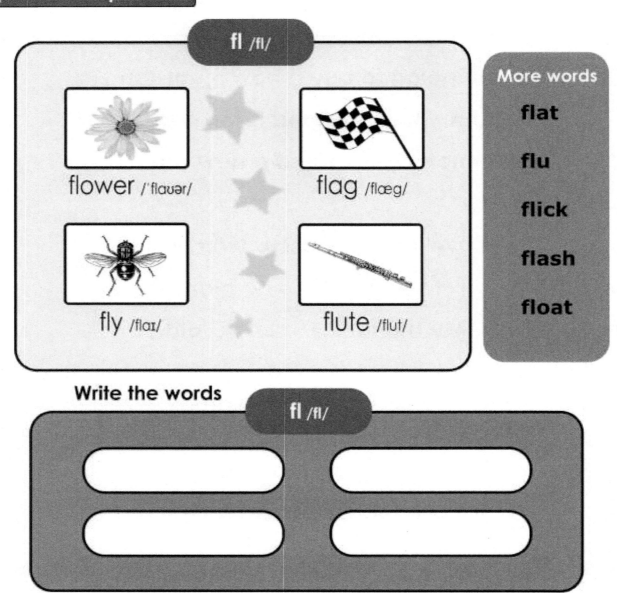

fl /fl/

flower /'flɑʊər/

flag /flæg/

fly /flɑɪ/

flute /flut/

More words

flat

flu

flick

flash

float

Write the words

fl /fl/

Write the letters & Read the sentences!

The _ _ower is _ _oating.

There is a _ _y on the _ _ute.

He _ _icked the _ _ame.

Complete the words

1. w_____e   3. m_____s   5. d_____s

2. b_____t   4. p_____w   6. n_____d

Write the answer next to the letter "A"

A: ___ **7.** Why are you ___ shopping now?

a. go
b. going
c. going to

A: ___ **8.** I'm going shopping because I need a new ___.

a. bed
b. bed sheets
c. drawers

A: ___ **9.** Are you going to buy a new alarm clock?

a. No, I'm not. I need a new one.
b. No, I'm not. I don't need new ones.
c. No I'm not. I don't need a new one.

A: ___ **10.** Are you going to buy ___ bed sheets?

a. a new
b. new
c. old

Answers on Page 306

- Learn the words
- Learn the sentences
- Learn the phonics
- Test yourself!

More places

додаткові місця

Learn the words

1. school школа	**6. factory** фабрика, завод
2. library бібліотека	**7. office** офіс
3. police station міліція	**8. fire station** пожежне депо
4. hospital лікарня	**9. clinic** поліклініка
5. train station залізнична станція	**10. bus stop** автобусна зупинка

Write the missing letters!

1. s_h_o_

2. l_b_ar_

3. p_l_ _e s_at_o_

4. h_sp_ _a_

5. tr_ _n s_a_i_n

6. f_c_o_y

7. o_fi_ _

8. f_ _e _t_o_

9. c_i_i_

10. b_ _ s_o_

Have fun with the words!

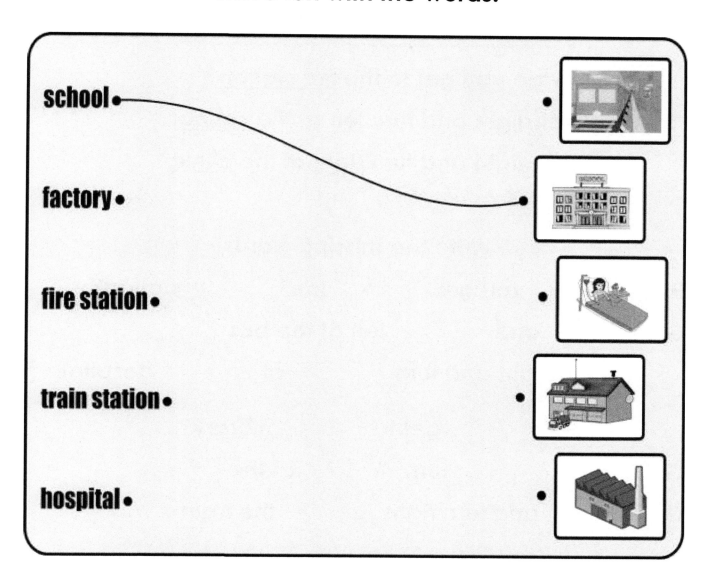

Write 4 more places!

1. _____   3. _____

2. _____   4. _____

How do you get to the bus stop?

_____

How do you get to the <u>fire station</u>?

Go straight and turn <u>left</u> at the <u>school</u>.

Go straight and turn <u>right</u> at the <u>clinic</u>.

Write the missing words!

How _____ you get _____ the _____ station?

Go _____ and _____ left at the bus _____ .

_____ straight and turn _____ at _____ hospital.

_____ do _____ get to _____ library?

Go straight _____ turn _____ at the _____ .

Go _____ and turn right _____ the train _____ .

How _____ you _____ _____ _____ clinic?

_____ straight and _____ left at the fire _____ .

Go _____ and turn _____ at the _____ .

_____ ?

_____ .

_____ .

Do you know how to get to the <u>bus stop</u>?

Yes, go straight and turn <u>right</u> at the <u>factory</u>.

No, I don't know how to get there.

Write the missing words!

Do you _____ how to _____ to the _____ stop?

Yes, go straight _____ turn _____ at the _____ .

_____ , I _____ know how to _____ there.

Do _____ know _____ to get to the _____ station?

_____ , go _____ and _____ left at the fire _____ .

No, _____ don't know _____ to get _____ .

_____ you _____ how to _____ to _____ clinic?

Yes, go _____ and _____ right _____ the hospital.

No, I _____ _____ how _____ _____ there.

_____ ?

_____ .

_____ .

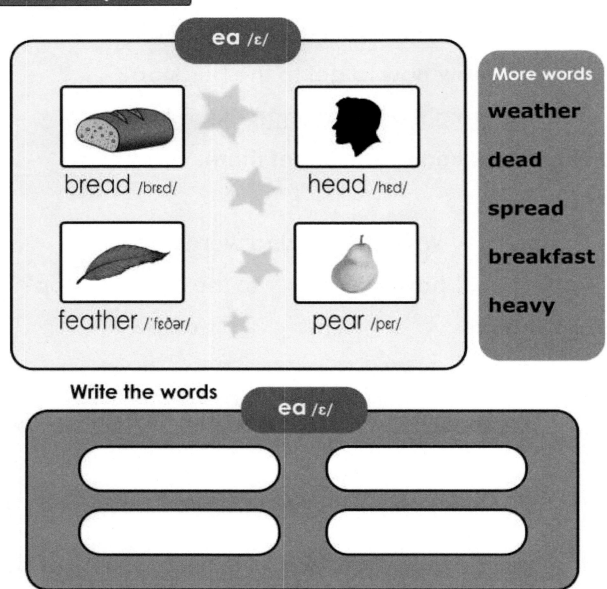

ea /ɛ/

bread /brɛd/

head /hɛd/

feather /ˈfɛðər/

pear /pɛr/

More words

weather

dead

spread

breakfast

heavy

Write the words

ea /ɛ/

Write the letters & Read the sentences!

We ate a p_ _r for br_ _kfast.

The f_ _ther is not h_ _vy.

I spr_ _d honey on my br_ _d.

Complete the words

1. b_____p 3. c_____c 5. l_____y

2. h_____l 4. p_____n 6. f_____y

Write the answer next to the letter "A"

A: ___ **7.** How do you get to the train station?

a. Go straight and turn left at school.
b. Go straight and turn left at the school.
c. Get straight and turn right at the school.

A: ___ **8.** Go straight and ___ the fire station.

a. turn right into
b. turn right to
c. turn right at

A: ___ **9.** Do you know ___ get to the office?

a. how
b. how to
c. why to

A: ___ **10.** No, I don't know how to get ___.

a. there
b. their
c. here

Answers on Page 306

Lesson
41
- Learn the words
- Learn the sentences
- Learn the phonics
- Test yourself!

The face

обличчя

Learn the words

1. **chin**
   підборіддя

2. **nose**
   ніс

3. **eye**
   око

4. **eyebrow**
   брова

5. **eyelash**
   вія

6. **ear**
   вухо

7. **hair**
   волосся

8. **cheek**
   щока

9. **mouth**
   рот

10. **lip**
    губа

Write the missing letters!

1. c_i_

2. _o_e

3. e_ _

4. e_eb_o_

5. ey_l_s_

6. _a_

7. h_ _r

8. c_e_ _

9. m_u_ _

10. l_ _

Have fun with the words!

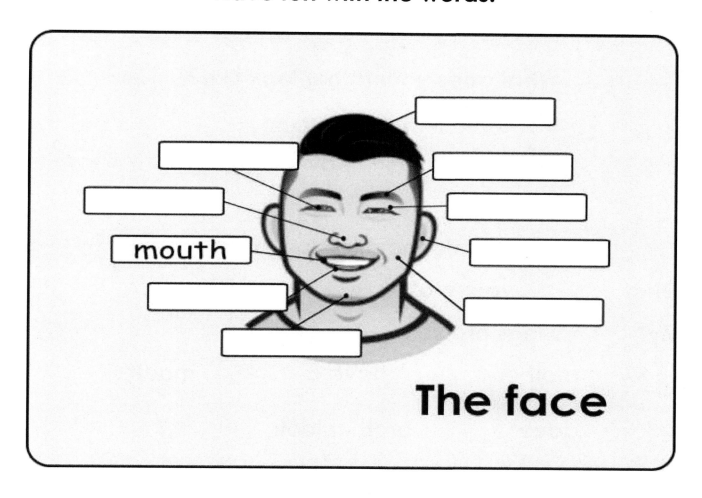

mouth

The face

Unscramble the letters!

1. UTOHM _____

2. ELSAYEH _____

3. RIHA _____

4. HICN _____

5. SONE _____

What does your <u>father</u> look like?

My father has <u>brown</u> <u>eye</u>s.

My father doesn't have a <u>big</u> <u>nose</u>.

Write the missing words!

What _____ your mother _____ like?

My _____ has brown _____ .

_____ mother _____ have a _____ mouth.

_____ does _____ brother look _____ ?

My brother _____ a _____ chin.

My _____ doesn't _____ blue _____ .

What _____ your _____ look _____ ?

My _____ has _____ eyelashes.

_____ aunt _____ _____ a small _____ .

_____ ?

_____ .

_____ .

Does your <u>sister</u> have <u>long</u> <u>hair</u>?

Yes, she does.

No, she has <u>short</u> hair.

Write the missing words!

Does _____ uncle _____ big cheeks?

Yes, he _____ .

No, he _____ small _____ .

_____ your grandmother _____ green _____ ?

Yes, _____ .

_____ , she has _____ eyes.

Does _____ grandfather _____ a small _____ ?

Yes, _____ _____ .

_____ , _____ has _____ big nose.

_____ ?

_____ .

_____ .

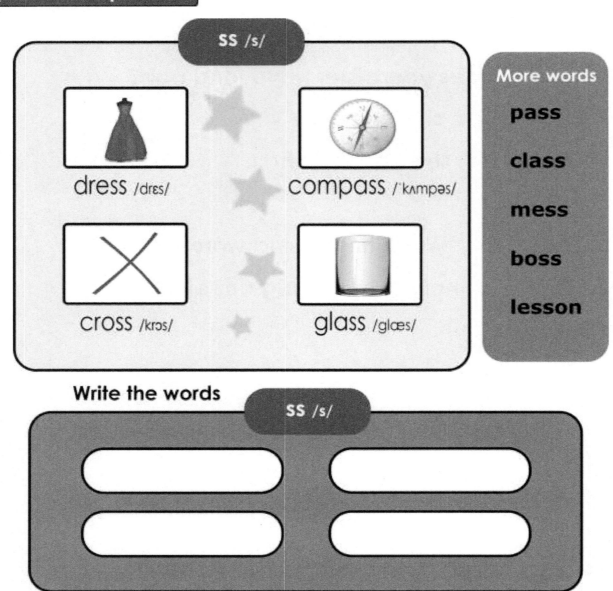

SS /s/

dress /drɛs/   compass /ˈkʌmpəs/

cross /krɔs/   glass /glæs/

More words

pass

class

mess

boss

lesson

Write the words

SS /s/

Write the letters & Read the sentences!

She wore a dre_ _ in cla_ _.

This le_ _on is about how to use a compa_ _.

My bo_ _ gave me this gla_ _.

Complete the words

1. e_____w   3. m_____h   5. c_____k

2. h_____r   4. n_____e   6. e_____h

Write the answer next to the letter "A"

A: ___ **7.** What ___ your uncle look ___?

a. do, likes
b. does, like
c. did, liked

A: ___ **8.** My mother ___ long hair.

a. have
b. doesn't have
c. don't have

A: ___ **9.** Does your brother have blue eyes?

a. No, she has green eyes.
b. No, he have green eyes.
c. No, he has green eyes.

A: ___ **10.** Does your grandfather ___?

a. have a big nose
b. have big nose
c. has a big nose

Answers on Page 306

Lesson 42

- Learn the words
- Learn the sentences
- Learn the phonics
- Test yourself!

Personalities

риси характеру

Learn the words

1. **shy**
сором'язливий

2. **lazy**
лінивий

3. **outgoing**
товариський

4. **generous**
щедрий

5. **studious**
старанний

6. **interesting**
цікавий

7. **serious**
серйозний

8. **funny**
забавний

9. **smart**
розумний

10. **easygoing**
добродушно-веселий

Write the missing letters!

1. s_ _

2. l_z_

3. o_t_oi_ _

4. _e_e_o_s

5. s_u_i_u_

6. in_e_es_i_g

7. s_r_o_s

8. f_n_ _

9. s_a_ _

10. e_s_g_i_g

Have fun with the words!

shy
lazy
outgoing
generous
studious
interesting
serious
funny
smart
easygoing

s
m
a
r
t

Write the missing word:

What is your <u>friend</u> like?

My friend is a really <u>outgoing</u> person.

My friend isn't a <u>shy</u> person.

Write the missing words!

What _____ your father _____?

My father is a _____ easygoing _____.

My father _____ a _____ person.

_____ is _____ sister like?

My _____ is _____ really _____ person.

_____ sister isn't _____ studious _____.

What _____ your _____?

_____ grandfather _____ a _____ smart _____.

My _____ a _____ _____.

_____?

_____.

_____.

Is your <u>mother</u> an <u>easygoing</u> person?

Yes, my mother is really easygoing.

No, my mother isn't easygoing.

Write the missing words!

Is _____ brother _____ interesting _____?

Yes, _____ brother is _____ interesting.

No, my _____ isn't _____.

_____ your _____ a _____ person?

_____, my aunt _____ really generous.

No, _____ aunt _____ generous.

Is _____ friend _____ studious _____?

Yes, _____ friend _____ really _____.

_____, my _____ isn't _____.

_____?

_____.

_____.

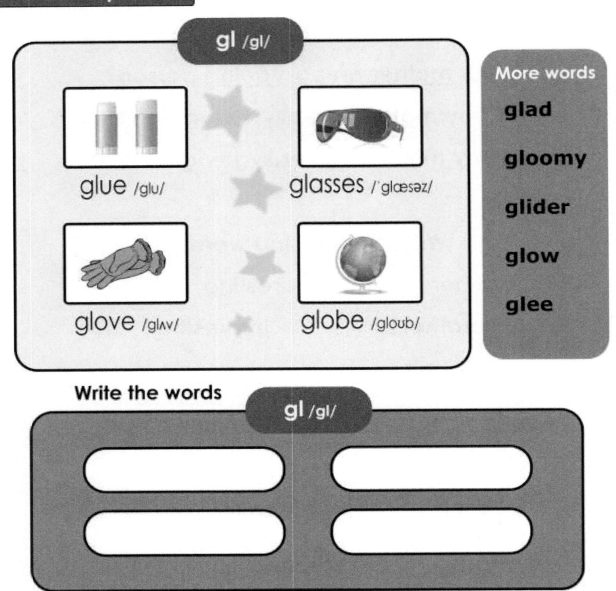

gl /gl/

glue /glu/

glasses /ˈglæsəz/

glove /glʌv/

globe /gloub/

More words

glad

gloomy

glider

glow

glee

Write the words

gl /gl/

Write the letters & Read the sentences!

I'm _ _ad I brought my _ _ider.

I can fix the _ _obe with _ _ue.

These _ _oves are _ _owing.

Complete the words

1. l_____y   3. g_____s   5. s_____t

2. o_____g   4. i_____g   6. e_____g

Write the answer next to the letter "A"

A: ___ **7.** What is your father like?

a. My father is really serious. My father isn't outgoing.
b. My father is real serious. My father isn't outgoing.
c. My father is really serious. My father is'nt outgoing.

A: ___ **8.** What ___ your grandmother like? My grandmother is really shy.

a. does
b. is
c. do

A: ___ **9.** Is your mother an ___ person? No, my mother is a ___ person.

a. easygoing, outgoing
b. lazy, studious
c. easygoing, smart

A: ___ **10.** Is your brother a funny person?

a. Yes, my brother isn't really funny.
b. Yes, me brother is really funny.
c. Yes, my brother is really funny.

Answers on Page 306

- Learn the words
- Learn the sentences
- Learn the phonics
- Test yourself!

Music

музика

Learn the words

1. **beautifully**
красиво

2. **quietly**
тихо

3. **slowly**
повільно

4. **gracefully**
витончено

5. **well**
добре

6. **loudly**
гучно

7. **quickly**
швидко

8. **terribly**
жахливо

9. **correctly**
правильно

10. **badly**
погано

Write the missing letters!

1. **be_u_if_l_y**

2. **_u_e_l_**

3. **sl_w_ _**

4. **g_a_e_u_l_**

5. **w_l_**

6. **l_ _d_y**

7. **q_i_k_y**

8. **_er_i_ly**

9. **c_r_ _c_l_**

10. **b_d_ _**

Have fun with the words!

Write the 3 missing words

1. _____

2. _____

3. _____

beautifully

well

terribly

quickly

slowly

badly

quietly

---

1. _____

2. _____

3. _____

quickly

gracefully

terribly

slowly

loudly

badly

correctly

---

1. _____

2. _____

3. _____

slowly

loudly

quietly

gracefully

well

correctly

badly

---

1. _____

2. _____

3. _____

quietly

correctly

quickly

loudly

gracefully

badly

beautifully

---

1. _____

2. _____

3. _____

well

gracefully

terribly

correctly

quietly

slowly

beautifully

---

1. _____

2. _____

3. _____

badly

correctly

quickly

well

loudly

terribly

slowly

How does he play the <u>violin</u>?

He plays the <u>violin</u> <u>beautifully</u>.

He doesn't play the <u>violin</u> <u>badly</u>.

Write the missing words!

How _____ he _____ the guitar?

He _____ the _____ quickly.

He _____ play _____ guitar _____ .

_____ does _____ play _____ drums?

She plays _____ drums _____ .

_____ doesn't _____ the _____ correctly.

How _____ he _____ the _____ ?

_____ plays _____ piano gracefully.

He _____ _____ piano _____ .

_____ ?

_____ .

_____ .

Does she play the <u>piano</u> <u>well</u>?

Yes, she plays the piano very well.

No, she doesn't. She plays the piano <u>terribly</u>.

Write the missing words!

Does she _____ the _____ loudly?

_____, she plays _____ drums _____ loudly.

No, _____ doesn't. She _____ the drums _____.

_____ he _____ the _____ gracefully?

Yes, _____ plays _____ violin very _____.

_____, he _____. He _____ the violin _____.

Does _____ play _____ guitar _____?

_____, she _____ the _____ _____ well.

No, _____ . She _____ the _____.

_____ ?

_____ .

_____ .

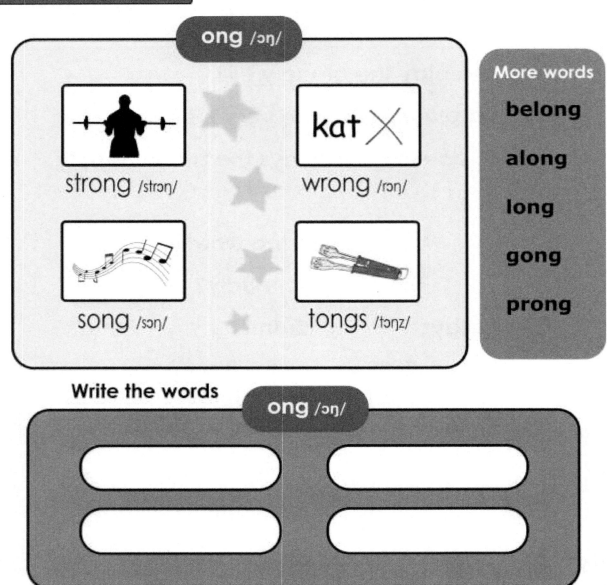

ong /ɔŋ/

strong /strɔŋ/

kat ✕ wrong /rɔŋ/

song /sɔŋ/

tongs /tɔŋz/

More words

belong

along

long

gong

prong

Write the words

ong /ɔŋ/

Write the letters & Read the sentences!

These t_ _ _s are too l_ _ _.

You can sing al_ _ _ to the s_ _ _.

This g_ _ _ bel_ _ _s to that str_ _ _ man.

Complete the words

1. s_____y   3. w_____l   5. c_____y

2. l_____y   4. g_____y   6. t_____y

Write the answer next to the letter "A"

A: ___ **7.** How ___ play the piano?

a. do he
b. does they
c. does she

A: ___ **8.** How does he play the guitar?

a. He play the guitar loudly.
b. He plays the guitar badly.
c. He plays the guitar correct.

A: ___ **9.** Does she ___ the violin well? Yes, she ___ the violin very well.

a. plays, plays
b. play, plays
c. plays, play

A: ___ **10.** Does he play the drums quietly?

a. No, he doesn't. He plays the drums loudly.
b. No, he don't. He plays the drums loudly.
c. No, he doesn't. He play the drums loudly.

Answers on Page 306

Activities

діяльность

Learn the words

1. **play piano**
   грати на піаніно

2. **read books**
   читати книги

3. **play video games**
   грати у відео ігри

4. **surf the internet**
   шукати в Інтернеті

5. **take photographs**
   Фотографувати

6. **watch TV**
   дивитись телевізор

7. **sing songs**
   співати пісні

8. **study English**
   вивчати англійську

9. **play cards**
   грати в карти

10. **go shopping**
    ходити за покупками

Write the missing letters!

1. p_a_ p_ _n_

2. r_ _d b_o_s

3. _la_ v_d_o g_ _e_

4. s_ _f t_e i_t_r_e_

5. t_k_ p_ot_g_a_hs

6. w_t_h T_

7. s_ _g s_n_s

8. s_u_y E_ _l_s_

9. _l_y c_ _ds

10. g_ s_op_i_g

Have fun with the words!

Connect the words

play •   • shopping

surf •   • cards

sing •   • photographs

go •   • the internet

watch •   • books

play •   • English

take •   • piano

study •   • songs

read •   • TV

Which activity is missing? _____

What have you been doing these days?

These days, I have been <u>reading books</u>.

I haven't been <u>singing songs</u>.

Write the missing words!

What _____ you _____ doing _____ days?

These _____, I've been _____ the internet.

I _____ been taking _____.

What have you been _____ these _____?

These days, we've _____ _____ video _____.

_____ haven't _____ going _____.

_____ have they _____ doing _____ _____?

These days, _____ been _____ English.

They _____ _____ watching _____.

_____ ?

_____ .

_____ .

Have you been <u>playing piano</u>?

Yes, I have been.

No, I haven't been.

Write the missing words!

Have _____ been _____ cards?

Yes, _____ have _____ .

_____ , I _____ been.

_____ you _____ going _____ ?

_____ , we _____ been.

No, _____ haven't _____ .

Have _____ been _____ books?

Yes, they _____ .

_____ , they _____ .

_____ ?

_____ .

_____ .

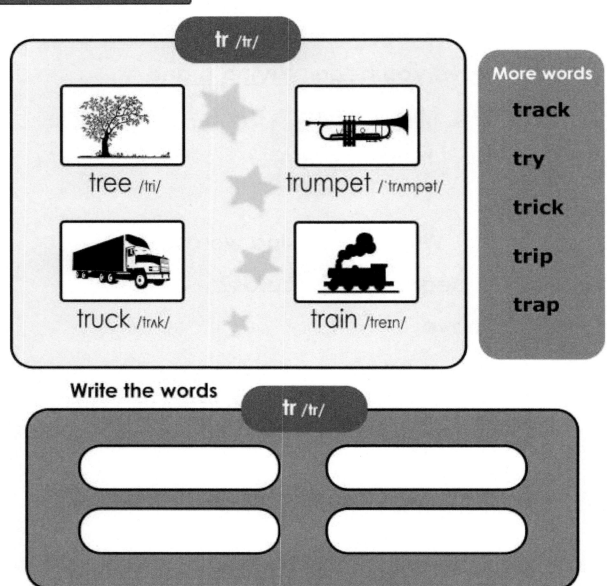

tr /tr/

tree /tri/

trumpet /'trʌmpət/

truck /trʌk/

train /treɪn/

More words

track

try

trick

trip

trap

Write the words

tr /tr/

Write the letters & Read the sentences!

The _ _ain is on the _ _ack.

I _ _ied to learn the _ _umpet.

We saw many _ _ucks on our _ _ip.

Complete the words

1. E____h   3. b____s   5. p____s

2. s____s   4. s____g   6. i____t

Write the answer next to the letter "A"

A: ___ **7.** What have you ___ doing lately?

a. be
b. been
c. being

A: ___ **8.** These days, I have been ___ video games.

a. playing
b. played
c. play

A: ___ **9.** Have you been watching TV?

a. Yes, I have.
b. Yes, I have been.
c. Yes, I been.

A: ___ **10.** ___ you been reading books? No, I ___ been.

a. Has, hasn't
b. Have, haven't
c. Are, aren't

Answers on Page 306

Lesson 45

- Learn the words
- Learn the sentences
- Learn the phonics
- Test yourself!

Outdoor activities

заходи на свіжому повітрі

Learn the words

1. kayaking
каякінг

2. going camping
відправлятися в похід з палатками

3. flying a kite
запускати повітряного змія

4. riding a horse
їздити верхи

5. going hiking
відправлятися в піший похід

6. skydiving
Затяжні стрибки з парашутом

7. riding a bike
кататись на велосипеді

8. snowboarding
сноубордінг

9. going fishing
рибалити

10. doing gardening
займатися садівництвом

Write the missing letters!

1. k_ya_i_g

2. g_i_g c_m_ _ng

3. f_y_ _g a _it_

4. r_ _i_g a h_ _s_

5. g_i_g h_ _i_g

6. s_y_i_i_g

7. r_d_n_ a b_ _e

8. s_o_b_a_di_g

9. _o_ng fi_h_n_

10. d_i_ _g_ _d_ni_g

Have fun with the words!

1. been / a / has / bike / She / spring / riding / this

_____ .

2. doing / winter / been / this / What / he / has

_____ ?

3. kite / hasn't / a / flying / He / been

_____ .

4. she / Has / gardening / been / autumn / this / doing

_____ ?

5. horse / a / been / riding / He's

_____ .

6. she / What / been / winter / has / this / doing

_____ ?

7. been / hasn't / No / she

_____ .

8. he / summer / this / going / been / Has / fishing

_____ ?

What has she been doing this <u>summer</u>?

She has been <u>riding a bike</u> this summer.

She hasn't been <u>flying a kite</u>.

Write the missing words!

What _____ he been _____ this winter?

He has _____ snowboarding this _____.

He _____ been _____ a horse.

_____ has _____ been doing this _____?

She _____ been _____ gardening _____ autumn.

She _____ _____ skydiving.

What _____ he _____ _____ _____ spring?

_____ has _____ going _____ this _____.

He _____ _____ _____ fishing.

_____ ?

_____ .

_____ .

Has he been <u>going hiking</u> this <u>spring</u>?

Yes, he has been.

No, he hasn't been. He's been <u>riding a horse</u>.

Write the missing words!

Has she _____ kayaking _____ summer?

_____, she _____ been.

No, _____ hasn't _____. She's been _____ a bike.

_____ he been _____ hiking _____ winter?

Yes, he _____ _____.

No, he _____ been. _____ _____ snowboarding.

Has _____ been _____ fishing _____ _____?

_____, she _____ _____.

No, _____ hasn't _____. She's been _____ a kite.

_____?

_____.

_____.

igh /aɪ/

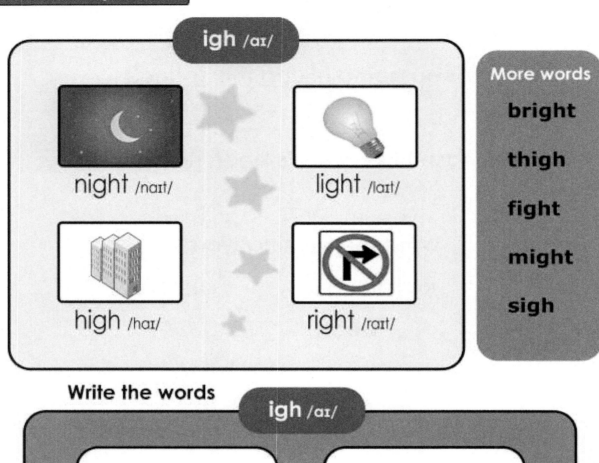

night /naɪt/

light /laɪt/

high /haɪ/

right /raɪt/

More words

bright

thigh

fight

might

sigh

Write the words

igh /aɪ/

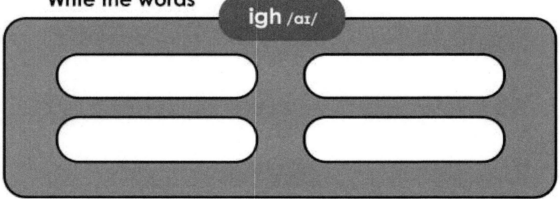

Write the letters & Read the sentences!

We leave the br_ _ _t l_ _ _ts on at n_ _ _t.

This table m_ _ _t be too h_ _ _.

My th_ _ _ is hurting on the r_ _ _t side.

Complete the words

1. h _____ e   3. c _____ g   5. g _____ g

2. f _____ g   4. k _____ g   6. k _____ e

Write the answer next to the letter "A"

A: ___ **7.** What ___ he been ___ this winter?

a. has, done
b. have, do
c. has, doing

A: ___ **8.** She has been ___ a kite this autumn.

a. flew
b. flying
c. flown

A: ___ **9.** Has she been kayaking this summer?

a. Yes, she has been.
b. Yes, she have been.
c. Yes, she has.

A: ___ **10.** Has he been snowboarding this winter?

a. No, he hasn't be. He's been skydiving.
b. No, he hasn't been. His been skydiving.
c. No, he hasn't been. He's been skydiving.

Answers on Page 306

Lesson
46
- Learn the words
- Learn the sentences
- Learn the phonics
- Test yourself!

Ocean life

життя в океані

Learn the words

1. dolphin дельфін	**6. jellyfish** медуза
2. seal тюлень	**7. tuna** тунець
3. whale кит	**8. salmon** лосось
4. octopus восьминіг	**9. crab** краб
5. shark акула	**10. squid** кальмар

Write the missing letters!

1. d_l_h_n

2. s_ _l

3. w_a_e

4. o_t_p_s

5. s_a_ _

6. j_l_y_i_h

7. t_n_

8. s_l_ _n

9. c_ _b

10. s_ _i_

Have fun with the words!

Find the 8 ocean animals!

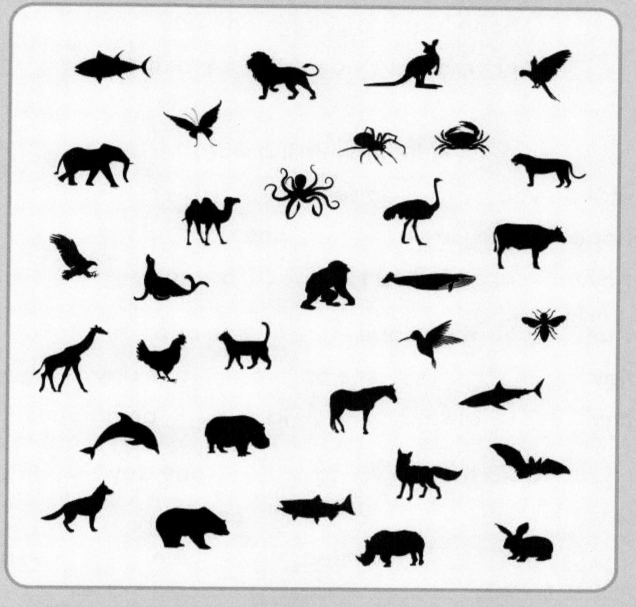

Write the 8 shapes

1.	3.	5.	7.
2.	4.	6.	8.

What do you hope to see one day?

I hope to see a <u>dolphin</u> one day.

I have always wanted to see a dolphin.

Write the missing words!

What do you _____ to see _____ day?

I hope _____ see a _____ one day.

I have _____ wanted to _____ a whale.

What _____ they hope _____ see one _____?

They _____ _____ see an _____ one day.

They _____ always _____ to _____ an octopus.

_____ does he _____ to _____ one day?

He _____ to _____ a _____ one _____.

_____ has _____ wanted _____ see _____ seal.

_____?

_____.

_____.

Have you ever seen a <u>shark</u>?

Yes, I have. I saw one in the ocean.

No, I have never seen a shark.

Write the missing words!

Have you _____ seen _____ jellyfish?

_____, I have. I _____ one in the _____.

No, I have _____ seen a _____.

Has she _____ seen a _____?

Yes, she _____. She saw _____ in _____ ocean.

_____, she has never _____ _____ seal.

_____ you ever _____ _____ salmon?

Yes, we _____. We _____ one _____ the _____.

No, _____ have _____ _____ a _____.

_____ ?

_____ .

_____ .

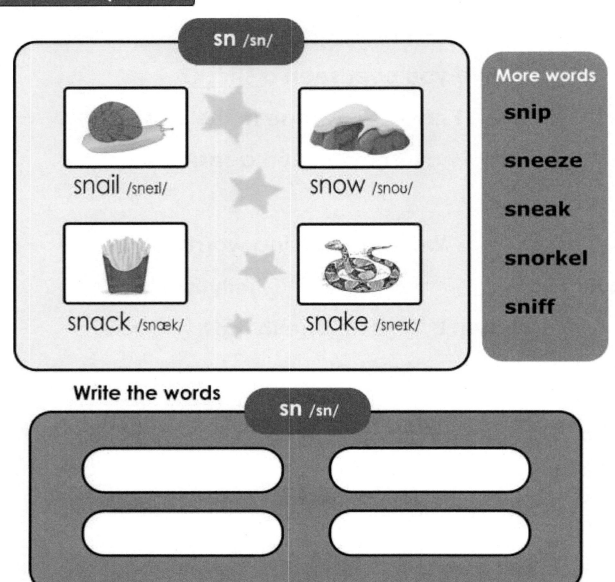

sn /sn/

snail /sneɪl/

snow /snoʊ/

snack /snæk/

snake /sneɪk/

More words

snip

sneeze

sneak

snorkel

sniff

Write the words

sn /sn/

Write the letters & Read the sentences!

He has been _ _iffing and _ _eezing.

There aren't any _ _ails in the _ _ow.

The _ _ake ate my _ _ack.

Complete the words

1. d_____n

3. o_____s

5. s_____d

2. j_____h

4. c_____b

6. t_____a

Write the answer next to the letter "A"

A: ___ **7.** What ___ she ___ see one day?

a. do, hope
b. does, hope to
c. does, hopes

A: ___ **8.** He has always ___ see a seal.

a. want to
b. wants to
c. wanted to

A: ___ **9.** ___ he ever seen a salmon?

a. Have
b. Has
c. Haves

A: ___ **10.** Have you ever seen a whale?

a. Yes, I have. I saw one in the ocean.
b. Yes, I have. I seen one in the ocean.
c. Yes, I have. I saw one at the ocean.

Answers on Page 306

- Learn the words
- Learn the sentences
- Learn the phonics
- Test yourself!

In the bathroom

у ванні

Learn the words

1. **shower**
душ

2. **bathtub**
ванна

3. **bath towel**
рушник

4. **bath mat**
килимок для ванної

5. **mirror**
дзеркало

6. **toilet**
туалет

7. **toilet paper**
туалетний папір

8. **sink**
раковина

9. **soap**
мило

10. **shelf**
полиця

Write the missing letters!

1. s_o_e_

2. b_t_t_b

3. _a_h t_ _e_

4. b_ _h m_ _

5. m_r_o_

6. t_ _le_

7. t_i_e_ p_p_ _

8. s_ _k

9. s_a_

10. s_e_ _

Have fun with the words!

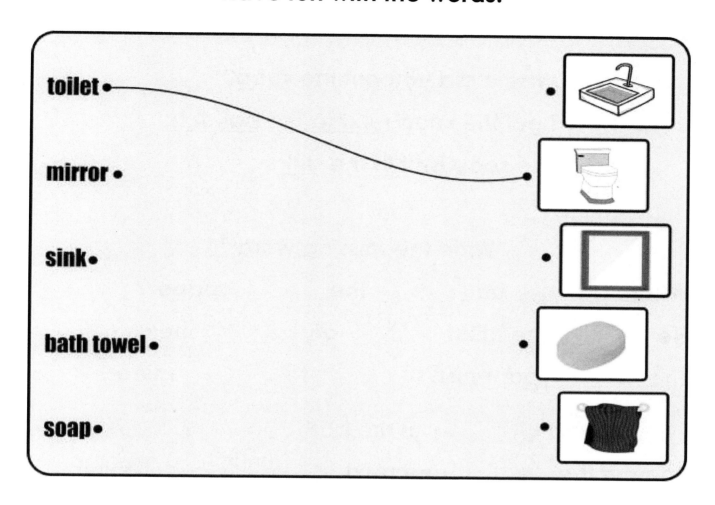

Unscramble the letters!

1. LHESF

2. TBHA MTA

3. HREWOS

4. LTOETI APREP

5. TBHUBTA

Where did you put the <u>soap</u>?

I put the soap <u>next to</u> the <u>bathtub</u>.

The soap isn't <u>in</u> the <u>sink</u>.

Write the missing words!

Where _____ he _____ the _____ paper?

He _____ the toilet _____ on _____ shelf.

The _____ paper isn't _____ to _____ mirror.

_____ did _____ put the bath _____?

She put the _____ mat next _____ _____ toilet.

The _____ _____ isn't in _____ bathtub.

Where _____ you _____ _____ _____?

I _____ the soap _____ the _____.

_____ soap _____ _____ _____ shower.

_____?

_____.

_____.

Did you put the <u>bath towel</u> <u>on</u> the <u>shelf</u>?

Yes, I did.

No, I didn't. I put it <u>next to</u> the <u>toilet</u>.

Write the missing words!

Did _____ put the _____ mat next to _____ sink?

Yes, she _____.

No, _____ didn't. She _____ it _____ the bathtub.

Did he _____ the _____ paper on _____ shelf?

Yes, _____ did.

No, he _____. _____ put it _____ the shower.

_____ you put the soap _____ to _____ mirror?

Yes, _____ _____.

_____, I _____. I put _____ in _____ _____.

_____?

_____.

_____.

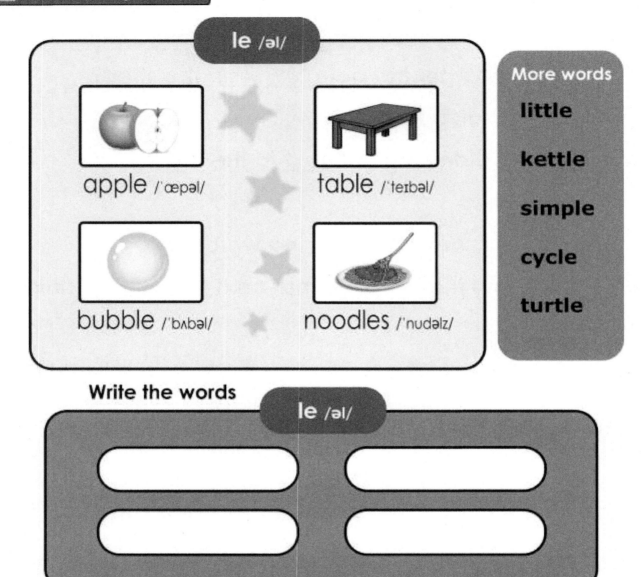

le /əl/

apple /ˈæpəl/

table /ˈteɪbəl/

bubble /ˈbʌbəl/

noodles /ˈnudəlz/

More words

little

kettle

simple

cycle

turtle

Write the words

le /əl/

Write the letters & Read the sentences!

I put the app_ _ on the tab_ _.

The turt_ _ looked at the bubb_ _.

This black kett_ _ is too litt_ _.

Complete the words

1. m_____r   3. b_____b   5. s_____f

2. t_____t   4. s_____r   6. s_____p

Write the answer next to the letter "A"

A: ___ **7.** Where did you put the bath towel?

a. I put the bath towel next too the shower.
b. I put the bath towel next the shower.
c. I put the bath towel next to the shower.

A: ___ **8.** The bath mat ___ in the bathroom.

a. doesn't
b. isn't
c. aren't

A: ___ **9.** Did she put the soap in the sink?

a. No, she didn't. She put it on the shelf.
b. No, he didn't. He put it on the shelf.
c. No she didn't. She put it on the shelf.

A: ___ **10.** Did he ___ the bath towel on the shelf?

a. puts
b. put
c. putting

Answers on Page 306

Lesson 48

- Learn the words
- Learn the sentences
- Learn the phonics
- Test yourself!

Capital cities

столиці

Learn the words

1. **London**
Лондон

2. **Madrid**
Мадрид

3. **Paris**
Париж

4. **Ottawa**
Оттава

5. **Washington, D.C.**
Вашингтон

6. **Cape Town**
Кейптаун

7. **Wellington**
Веллінгтон

8. **Canberra**
Канберра

9. **Bangkok**
Бангкок

10. **Beijing**
Пекін

Write the missing letters!

1. L_n_o_

2. _a_r_d

3. P_ _i_

4. O_t_ _a

5. _a_ _in_to_, D. _.

6. C_p_ T_ _n

7. _e_li_g_o_

8. C_ _be_r_

9. _a_g_ _k

10. B_ _j_n_

Have fun with the words!

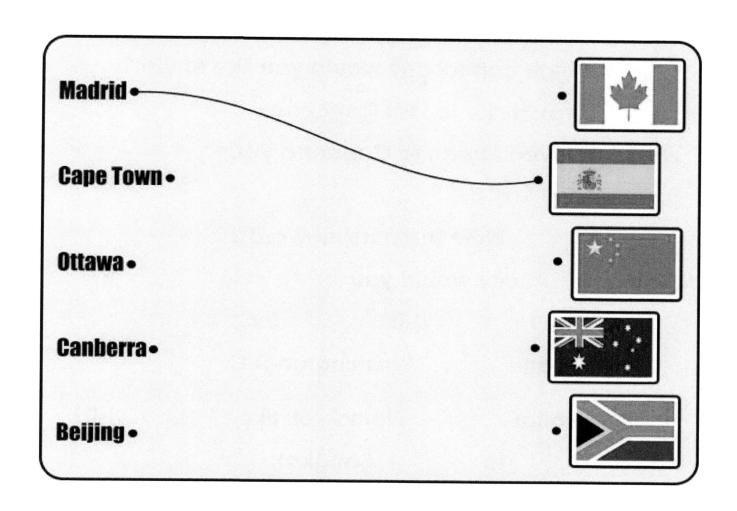

Madrid •

Cape Town •

Ottawa •

Canberra •

Beijing •

Write 4 more capital cities!

1. _____

2. _____

3. _____

4. _____

What is the capital city of your country?

_____

Which capital city would you like to visit?

I would like to visit <u>Canberra</u>.

I haven't been to Canberra yet.

Write the missing words!

Which _____ city would you _____ to _____ ?

I _____ like _____ visit _____ D.C.

I _____ been _____ Washington D.C. _____ .

_____ capital _____ would you like _____ visit?

I would _____ to _____ Bangkok.

_____ haven't _____ to _____ yet.

Which _____ _____ would _____ like to _____ ?

I _____ _____ to visit _____ Town.

I _____ _____ to Cape _____ _____ .

_____ ?

_____ .

_____ .

Would you like to visit <u>London</u>?

Yes, I would love to visit London.

No, I have already been there.

Write the missing words!

Would you _____ to _____ Paris?

Yes, I _____ love _____ visit _____.

No, _____ have _____ been _____.

_____ you like _____ visit _____?

Yes, _____ would _____ to _____ Ottawa.

_____, I _____ already _____ there.

Would _____ like _____ Beijing?

Yes, I _____ love _____.

_____, I _____ already _____.

_____?

_____.

_____.

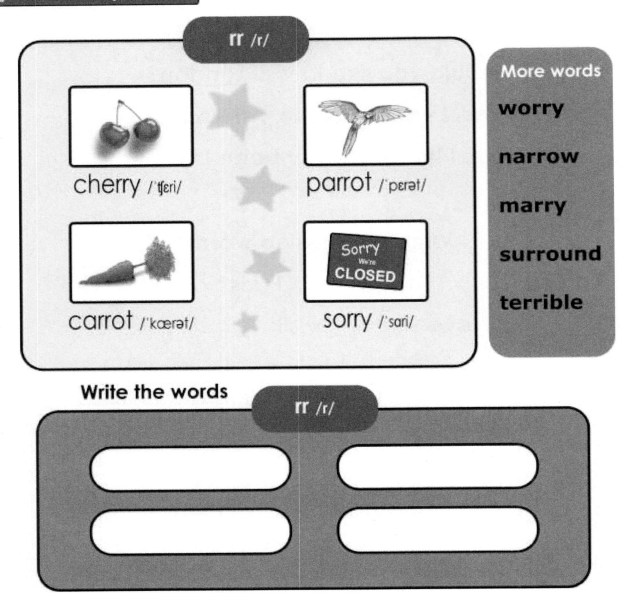

rr /r/

cherry /ˈtʃɛri/

parrot /ˈpɛrət/

carrot /ˈkærət/

sorry /ˈsɑri/

More words

worry

narrow

marry

surround

terrible

Write the words

rr /r/

Write the letters & Read the sentences!

That pa_ _ot eats che_ _ies.

I'm so_ _y I ate your ca_ _ot.

He is wo_ _ied about taking a fe_ _y.

Complete the words

1. P_____s   3. B_____k   5. C_____a

2. O_____a   4. W_____n   6. L_____n

Write the answer next to the letter "A"

A: ___ **7.** Which capital city ___ you like to visit?

a. would
b. could
c. should

A: ___ **8.** I ___ been to Washington D.C. yet.

a. have
b. haven't
c. hasn't

A: ___ **9.** Would you like to visit Cape Town?

a. Yes, I would to love visit Cape Town.
b. Yes, I would love to visit Cape Town.
c. Yes, I would love visiting Cape Town.

A: ___ **10.** No, I have ___ been there.

a. already
b. all ready
c. yet

Answers on Page 306

Lesson 49
- Learn the words
- Learn the sentences
- Learn the phonics
- Test yourself!

In the toolbox

в ящику для інструментів

Learn the words

1. **a hammer**
молоток

2. **a shovel**
лопата

3. **a paintbrush**
кисть

4. **a screwdriver**
викрутка

5. **an electric drill**
електрична дриль

6. **a tape measure**
рулетка

7. **a wrench**
гайковий ключ

8. **a ladder**
драбина

9. **pliers**
плоскогубці

10. **an axe**
сокира

Write the missing letters!

1. h_m_e_

2. s_o_ _l

3. p_ _n_b_u_h

4. s_r_w_r_v_r

5. _le_t_ _c d_i_l

6. t_ _e m_ _su_e

7. _r_n_h

8. l_d_ _r

9. _li_r_

10. a_ _

Have fun with the words!

➢ **Find one mistake and write the sentence correctly**

Which tool should I uses to fix the table?

_____

You should use a electric drill.

_____

You should'nt use a wrench.

_____

Which tool should I use fix the chair?

_____

You should use a pliers.

_____

You shouldn't use tape measure.

_____

Should I use an axe to fix these shelf?

_____

No, he should use a screwdriver.

_____

Which tool should I use to fix the <u>chair</u>?

You should use <u>a screwdriver</u>.

You shouldn't use <u>a hammer</u>.

Write the missing words!

Which _____ should I _____ to fix _____ table?

You _____ use an _____ drill.

_____ shouldn't _____ pliers.

_____ tool _____ I use _____ fix the shelf?

You should _____ _____ ladder.

You _____ _____ an _____ .

Which _____ _____ I _____ to _____ the chair?

_____ should _____ a tape _____ .

You _____ _____ _____ shovel.

_____?

_____.

_____.

Should I use <u>pliers</u> to fix the <u>table</u>?

Yes, you should.

No, you should use <u>a wrench</u>.

Write the missing words!

Should I _____ a screwdriver to _____ the _____?

Yes, you _____.

No, _____ should _____ an electric _____.

_____ I use _____ paintbrush to fix _____ shelf?

Yes, _____ should.

No, you _____ use _____ axe.

Should I _____ a hammer _____ fix _____ table?

Yes, _____ _____.

_____, you _____ use _____ _____ measure.

_____?

_____.

_____.

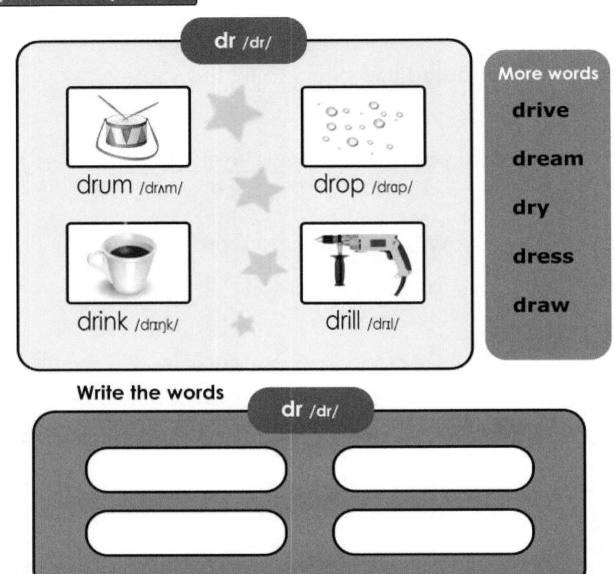

dr /dr/

drum /drʌm/

drop /drɑp/

drink /drɪŋk/

drill /drɪl/

More words

drive

dream

dry

dress

draw

Write the words

dr /dr/

Write the letters & Read the sentences!

My _ _eam is to play the _ _ums.

I _ _opped the _ _ink on your _ _ess.

The electric _ _ill is still not _ _y.

Complete the words

1. w_____h   3. s_____l   5. s_____r

2. h_____r   4. p_____s   6. p_____h

Write the answer next to the letter "A"

A: ___ **7.** Which tool should I use to fix the shelf?

a. You should use a axe to fix the shelf.
b. You should use an axe to fix the shelf.
c. You should use an axe fix the shelf.

A: ___ **8.** You ___ use a ladder.

a. shouldnt'
b. should'nt
c. shouldn't

A: ___ **9.** Should I use an ___ to fix the table?

a. electric drill
b. hammer
c. ladder

A: ___ **10.** Should I use a tape measure to fix the chair?

a. Yes, I should.
b. Yes, you should.
c. Yes, you did.

Answers on Page 306

Lesson 50

- Learn the words
- Learn the sentences
- Learn the phonics
- Test yourself!

At the cinema

в кінотеатрі

Learn the words

1. **exciting**
захоплюючий

2. **scary**
страшний

3. **romantic**
романтичний

4. **violent**
зі сценами насилля

5. **informative**
інформативний

6. **interesting**
цікавий

7. **boring**
нудний

8. **enjoyable**
приємний

9. **sad**
сумний

10. **funny**
смішний

Write the missing letters!

1. e_c_ti_g

2. s_a_ _

3. _o_a_t_c

4. v_ _l_n_

5. i_f_r_a_i_e

6. i_t_re_t_n_

7. _o_i_g

8. e_j_ _a_le

9. s_ _

10. f_n_ _

Have fun with the words!

Word Search

```
i  z  e  q  q  e  i  q  p  q  b  p  z  v  s  i  l  n
e  n  x  m  k  f  n  n  i  r  t  x  u  z  i  m  c  j
v  m  t  v  z  k  q  j  f  u  o  i  y  a  i  r  y  d
s  i  y  e  i  p  e  j  o  o  m  m  d  i  z  g  q  s
f  e  m  b  r  o  x  x  j  y  r  c  a  p  b  g  o  c
m  u  j  s  v  e  l  m  c  t  a  m  c  n  r  r  m  a
l  f  n  t  c  p  s  e  p  i  n  b  a  q  t  s  p  r
x  q  j  n  f  x  w  t  n  x  t  r  l  t  e  i  a  y
s  n  g  y  y  p  b  n  i  t  c  i  x  e  i  f  c  g
v  a  w  b  o  r  i  n  g  n  e  a  n  n  p  v  o  l
d  c  d  s  h  w  v  f  r  g  g  a  o  g  m  b  e  c
f  e  p  x  a  j  y  j  l  d  v  b  t  a  x  q  b  z
```

exciting	**interesting**
scary	**boring**
romantic	**enjoyable**
violent	**sad**
informative	**funny**

What did you think about the movie?

I thought the movie was <u>exciting</u>.

I didn't think the movie was <u>boring</u>.

Write the missing words!

What _____ you think _____ the _____?

I _____ the _____ was funny.

I didn't _____ the movie _____ _____.

_____ did he _____ about _____ movie?

He _____ _____ movie _____ scary.

He _____ think _____ _____ was enjoyable.

What _____ _____ think _____ the _____?

_____ thought _____ _____ was _____.

She _____ _____ the _____ _____ boring.

_____?

_____.

_____.

Did you think the movie was <u>romantic</u>?

Yes, I thought it was.

No, I thought it was <u>sad</u>.

Write the missing words!

Did you _____ the _____ was exciting?

Yes, _____ thought _____ was.

No, I _____ it was _____ .

Did _____ think _____ movie _____ informative?

_____ , she _____ it _____ .

No, _____ thought _____ was _____ .

_____ he _____ the _____ _____ boring?

Yes, _____ thought _____ _____ .

_____ , he _____ was _____ .

_____ ?

_____ .

_____ .

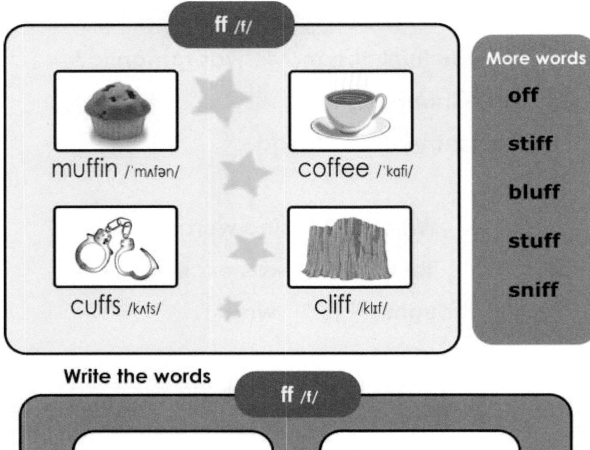

ff /f/

muffin /ˈmʌfən/

coffee /ˈkɑfi/

cuffs /kʌfs/

cliff /klɪf/

More words

off

stiff

bluff

stuff

sniff

Write the words

ff /f/

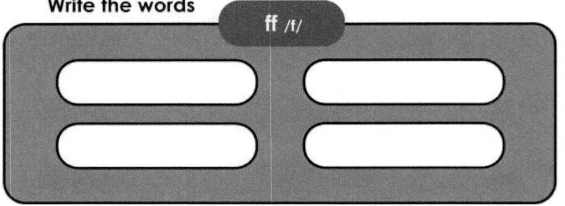

Write the letters & Read the sentences!

Don't fall o_ _ the cli_ _.

The dog is sni_ _ing the mu_ _ins.

These handcu_ _s are too sti_ _.

Complete the words

1. v_____t   3. f_____y   5. s_____y

2. r_____c   4. e_____e   6. e_____g

Write the answer next to the letter "A"

A: ___ **7.** What did you think about the movie?

a. I thought movie was sad. I didn't think movie was scary.
b. I thought the movie was sad. I didn't thought the movie was scary.
c. I thought the movie was sad. I didn't think the movie was scary.

A: ___ **8.** What did he think ___ the movie?

a. around
b. about
c. above

A: ___ **9.** Did you think the movie was informative?

a. Yes, I thought it was.
b. Yes, I thought it is.
c. Yes, I thought it did.

A: ___ **10.** Did she ___ the movie was informative?

a. think
b. thought
c. thinks

Answers on Page 306

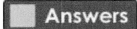**Answers**

Test 1-5	Lesson 1	Lesson 2	Lesson 3	Lesson 4	Lesson 5
Question 1	pencil	computer	yellow	brother	star
Question 2	tape	globe	brown	sister	triangle
Question 3	marker	poster	orange	uncle	octagon
Question 4	eraser	bookshelf	green	aunt	rectangle
Question 5	crayon	whiteboard	black	father	heart
Question 6	whiteout	desk	purple	mother	diamond
Question 7	c	a	b	b	b
Question 8	b	b	c	c	c
Question 9	a	c	a	b	a
Question 10	b	a	b	a	c

Test 6-10	Lesson 6	Lesson 7	Lesson 8	Lesson 9	Lesson 10
Question 1	tiger	builder	strawberry	stomach	tennis
Question 2	bear	nurse	cherry	head	volleyball
Question 3	monkey	salesclerk	watermelon	foot	golf
Question 4	kangaroo	doctor	pineapple	finger	cricket
Question 5	lion	teacher	banana	shoulder	badminton
Question 6	crocodile	chef	lemon	neck	hockey
Question 7	a	B	b	c	a
Question 8	c	c	a	b	c
Question 9	b	b	c	b	a
Question 10	b	a	c	a	b

Test 11-15	Lesson 11	Lesson 12	Lesson 13	Lesson 14	Lesson 15
Question 1	store	blouse	geography	carrot	airplane
Question 2	cinema	sweater	computer	potato	dinosaur
Question 3	park	necktie	history	broccoli	robot
Question 4	restaurant	jacket	music	spinach	teddy bear
Question 5	supermarket	scarf	English	mushroom	ball
Question 6	gym	dress	science	onion	doll
Question 7	b	b	a	b	c
Question 8	b	b	b	c	b
Question 9	c	a	b	a	a
Question 10	a	a	c	c	b

Test 16-20	Lesson 16	Lesson 17	Lesson 18	Lesson 19	Lesson 20
Question 1	blender	angry	strawberry	cloudy	clock
Question 2	stove	sad	raspberry	sunny	armchair
Question 3	pan	bored	chocolate	freezing	bookcase
Question 4	toaster	tired	vanilla	rainy	sofa
Question 5	cupboard	energetic	cherry	warm	television
Question 6	refrigerator	frustrated	almond	cold	painting
Question 7	a	a	c	c	b
Question 8	b	c	b	a	c
Question 9	a	a	c	c	c
Question 10	c	b	a	c	a

Test 21-25	Lesson 21	Lesson 22	Lesson 23	Lesson 24	Lesson 25
Question 1	laundry	rabbit	swim	beef	Australia
Question 2	carpet	hamster	sing	chicken	Germany
Question 3	clothes	snake	read	salami	Mexico
Question 4	floor	mouse	cook	shrimp	England
Question 5	bedroom	turtle	write	bacon	Japan
Question 6	dinner	bird	draw	sausage	Russia
Question 7	a	a	c	a	b
Question 8	c	b	b	b	c
Question 9	c	c	a	c	a
Question 10	b	c	b	c	b

Test 26-30	Lesson 26	Lesson 27	Lesson 28	Lesson 29	Lesson 30
Question 1	Portuguese	bread	cupcakes	music room	ferry
Question 2	Vietnamese	water	pudding	lunchroom	airplane
Question 3	Spanish	salad	apple pie	computer lab	subway
Question 4	Hindi	juice	brownies	nurse's office	motorcycle
Question 5	Arabic	meat	waffles	office	train
Question 6	French	cola	pastries	classroom	scooter
Question 7	b	b	c	b	c
Question 8	c	c	c	c	b
Question 9	c	a	a	b	b
Question 10	b	b	b	a	a

Test 31-35	Lesson 31	Lesson 32	Lesson 33	Lesson 34	Lesson 35
Question 1	doughnut	mountain	article	meeting	binoculars
Question 2	cheeseburger	beach	presentation	appointment	compass
Question 3	french fries	river	quiz	party	plastic dishes
Question 4	onion rings	jungle	workbook	recital	gas bottle
Question 5	pancake	ocean	speech	birthday	cooler
Question 6	burrito	waterfall	report	competition	barbecue
Question 7	c	b	c	b	c
Question 8	c	c	c	c	a
Question 9	c	a	b	a	c
Question 10	a	b	a	c	a

Test 36-40	Lesson 36	Lesson 37	Lesson 38	Lesson 39	Lesson 40
Question 1	trash	trash can	gardening	wardrobe	bus stop
Question 2	breakfast	stop sign	photographs	blanket	hospital
Question 3	shower	fire hydrant	karaoke	mattress	clinic
Question 4	shopping	police car	fishing	pillow	police station
Question 5	homework	ambulance	camping	drawers	library
Question 6	dinner	truck	hiking	nightstand	factory
Question 7	b	c	a	b	b
Question 8	c	b	b	a	c
Question 9	c	b	c	c	b
Question 10	b	a	c	b	a

Test 41-45	Lesson 41	Lesson 42	Lesson 43	Lesson 44	Lesson 45
Question 1	eyebrow	lazy	slowly	English	horse
Question 2	hair	outgoing	loudly	songs	fishing
Question 3	mouth	generous	well	books	camping
Question 4	nose	interesting	gracefully	shopping	kayaking
Question 5	cheek	smart	correctly	photographs	gardening
Question 6	eyelash	easygoing	terribly	internet	kite
Question 7	b	a	c	b	c
Question 8	b	b	b	c	b
Question 9	c	c	b	a	a
Question 10	a	c	a	c	c

Test 46-50	Lesson 46	Lesson 47	Lesson 48	Lesson 49	Lesson 50
Question 1	dolphin	mirror	Paris	wrench	violent
Question 2	jellyfish	toilet	Ottawa	hammer	romantic
Question 3	octopus	bathtub	Bangkok	shovel	funny
Question 4	crab	shower	Wellington	pliers	enjoyable
Question 5	squid	shelf	Canberra	screwdriver	scary
Question 6	tuna	soap	London	paintbrush	exciting
Question 7	b	c	a	b	c
Question 8	c	b	b	c	b
Question 9	b	a	b	a	a
Question 10	a	b	a	b	a

Printed in Great Britain
by Amazon

81763681R00176